OPPORTUNITIES

in

W9-DEV-014

Occupational Therapy Careers

REVISED EDITION

ZONA R. WEEKS

McGraw Hill

New York   Chicago   San Francisco   Lisbon   London   Madrid   Mexico City
Milan   New Delhi   San Juan   Seoul   Singapore   Sydney   Toronto

Library of Congress Cataloging-in-Publication Data

Weeks, Zona Roberta, 1936–
    Opportunities in occupational therapy careers / by Zona R. Weeks. — Rev. ed.
      p.   cm.
    Rev. ed. of: Opportunities in occupational therapy careers / Marguerite Abbott,
Marie-Louise Franciscus, Zona R. Weeks. c2001.
    Includes bibliographical references.
    ISBN 0-07-146770-X (alk. paper)
    1. Occupational therapy—Vocational guidance.   I. Abbott, Marguerite.
Opportunities in occupational therapy careers.   II. Title.
    [DNLM: 1. Occupational Therapy.   2. Vocational Guidance.
WB 555 W396o 2007]

    RM735.4.A22   2007
    615.8'515023—dc22   2005034473

3 4 5 6 7 8 9 10 11 12 13 14 15 16 17 18 19   DSH/DSH   0 9

ISBN-13: 978-0-07-146770-4
ISBN-10:   0-07-146770-X

Interior design by Rattray Design

McGraw-Hill books are available at special quantity discounts to use as premiums and
sales promotions, or for use in corporate training programs. For more information, please
write to the Director of Special Sales, Professional Publishing, McGraw-Hill, Two Penn
Plaza, New York, NY 10121-2298. Or contact your local bookstore.

This book is printed on acid-free paper.

This volume is dedicated to the occupational therapy students of the world—those who are, those who have been, and those who will be.

Contents

Foreword

Over the past decade, the demand for occupational therapy services has skyrocketed along with employment opportunities, salaries, and benefits. Some of this growth has come about as nearly every country in the world attempts to include individuals with disabilities in the workplace and the community. Practitioners in this field make valuable contributions to society in any number of ways. Occupational therapists and occupational therapy assistants are helping employers and business owners to make their premises more accessible and less likely to cause injury or disability. They also aid employers, employees, and those with disabilities in workplace integration for people with disabilities.

In America, occupational therapy services are a critical component of efforts to assist the growing number of people dealing with problems related to aging and for infants and children with problems associated with premature birth or birth defects. The many individuals surviving accidents and illness with significant difficulties in meeting their daily needs benefit from interventions offered by occupational therapy personnel.

Occupational therapy is based on the use of everyday activities as the means of helping people to achieve independence. Certified occupational therapy personnel consist of occupational therapists and occupational therapy assistants. The occupational therapy assistant completes a two-year associate degree program; the occupational therapist enters the field with a bachelor's degree or master's degree. Opportunities for advancement are many and varied, as are the types of disabling conditions, the ages of individuals who receive services, and the settings in which one might work. Many seek graduate education, opting to shift into roles of educator, researcher, consultant, administrator, or master clinician.

Employment and private enterprise opportunities in the field of occupational therapy are expanding and diversifying. Community and home-based programs offer personnel options to deliver direct primary health care, to conduct research, and to manage programs offering services to people with a wide variety of physical, emotional, and educational disabling conditions. Many more occupational therapists and occupational therapy assistants are needed in school systems. Those with an entrepreneurial spirit find private practice attractive.

Practitioners also enjoy the freedom to move from one work setting to another to meet changing personal and professional goals throughout their careers. Occupational therapists often manage treatment programs administered by a variety of individuals with differing educational preparation and professional credentials.

Occupational therapy's important role in our health-care system is likely to expand significantly as a result of reforms being developed in the United States. Working directly with clients in the home, community, school, and workplace using everyday activities people want and need to perform, occupational therapy practitioners improve the prospects of a satisfying, productive life for countless Americans.

Mary M. Evert, M.B.A., OTR, FAOTA
Former President
American Occupational Therapy Association

PREFACE

ACCORDING TO THE United States Department of Labor, occupational therapy is one of the fastest-growing health professions in the nation. In recent years the profession has undergone tremendous change and development, stimulated both from within and from societal pressures to fill specific health-care needs. At the initiative of practitioners, there has been an elaboration and clarification of the profession's underlying philosophies, frames of reference, and knowledge bases. Technological advances and increased knowledge, with development of new theoretical rationales and techniques for treatment, have resulted in increasingly effective health-care delivery. Occupational therapy has expanded to meet society's demands for health-care service in new areas for which occupational therapists have the necessary expertise. This expertise is acquired during educational preparation involving extensive academic work and supervised clinical experiences.

Contributions of occupational therapists to health-care delivery occur in the medical system (in hospitals or similar facilities) and in the community through various health-related agencies or health-promotion programs. The primary concern is to restore an individual to a functional state for return to society, if possible. In the community and in the educational system in particular, the emphasis is on normal development and promotion of optimum health and life-functioning abilities.

Today there is an air of excitement in the profession of occupational therapy as clinicians, administrators, educators, and students reach for new professional horizons. This small book can touch upon only some of the many aspects of occupational therapy that might interest future students. We hope that this book provides guidance and direction that will encourage the motivated reader to seek more detailed information and follow through with career education plans.

This edition has been revised to reflect some of the newer developments in the profession and to incorporate current educational program listings, salary levels, and other data.

Acknowledgments

We appreciate the assistance of staff members at the American Occupational Therapy Association, who provided important data used in this edition.

1

OVERVIEW OF THE PROFESSION

OCCUPATIONAL THERAPY, AS a health-care profession, is very well described by its name, with a focus on the word *occupation*. However, *occupation* has more than one meaning. It may refer to life occupations or roles, including not only work roles but also other roles in life such as preschooler, student, parent, and so forth. *Occupation* also refers to the process of doing (or occupying), and in occupational therapy it may be defined as tasks or activities with specific goals or purposes.

Occupational therapists attempt to minimize handicaps that have resulted from physical, developmental, cognitive, emotional, and social problems, and to help individuals obtain maximum independence. Skills for self-care, school or work, play or leisure, and interpersonal and group interactions are necessary for a satisfying, productive life. Developing new or lost skills is important, as is maintaining functional levels as long as possible in a person whose condition is declining. Quality of life and concern for the total individual are of prime importance. Occupational therapists realize that in dealing with human beings, one cannot separate mind from body. They often incorporate psychological knowledge and methods to help them understand and work with persons who have physical disabilities, and they would not overlook physical components in working with mentally ill patients.

Personal traits necessary for working in this profession are maturity, intelligence, imagination, patience, and teaching ability. The ability to solve problems is also important. Occupational therapists work to help patients or clients improve their functional level and seek their active participation in setting goals whenever possible.

The definition of occupational therapy accepted by the American Occupational Therapy Association Representative Assembly in 1981 is as follows:

> Occupational therapy is the use of purposeful activity with individuals who are limited by physical injury or illness, psychosocial dysfunction, developmental or learning disabilities, poverty and cultural differences or the aging process, in order to maximize independence, prevent disability, and maintain health. The practice encompasses evaluation, treatment and consultation. Specific occupational therapy services include teaching daily living skills; developing perceptual motor skills and sensory integrative functioning; developing play skills and prevocational and leisure capacities; designing, fabricating or applying selected orthotic and prosthetic devices or selective adaptive equipment; using specifically designed crafts and exercises to enhance functional performance; administering and interpreting tests such as manual muscle testing and range of motion; and adapting environments for the handicapped. These services are provided individually, in groups, or through social systems.

As you read the following chapters, many aspects of occupational therapy should become clear. To supplement the information that you gain from this book, it is a good idea to visit hospitals, schools, and other facilities to observe various types of occupational therapy practice.

Two levels of practice exist in the occupational therapy profession: the registered occupational therapist (OTR) and the certified occupational therapy assistant (COTA). Occupational therapists evaluate patients or clients, plan their programs, and supervise or provide treatment. Occupational therapy assistants work with occupational therapists in the planning and carrying out of treatment. While the majority of occupational therapists have entered the profession with a bachelor's degree in occupational therapy, in January 2007 the minimum educational standard will be an entry-level master's degree.

Occupational therapy assistants complete an associate degree program and generally gain the majority of their training on the job. Greater detail regarding educational requirements may be found in Chapter 4, and a list of educational programs at both levels may be found in Appendix A.

Patient or Client?

The terms *patient* and *client* are used to refer to persons receiving occupational therapy services. *Patient* is used in the medical system and *client* is more commonly used in the community system. Who is the patient or client? He or she may be a skilled worker who has lost the ability to work because of an accident; a child with learning disabilities caused by delayed development accompanied by sensory-integrative or perceptual problems; a homemaker confined to a wheelchair because of arthritis; a stroke victim who must learn to speak, dress, and feed herself or himself again; an emotionally troubled person who must acquire the confidence to reenter the working world; a birth-injured child with multiple problems involving speech, vision, and motor control; or an amputee who must learn to use a prosthesis. The list is endless, fascinating, and challenging. For our purposes, throughout this book the terms *patient* and *client* will be used interchangeably.

In 1962 the World Federation of Occupational Therapists put forth the functions of occupational therapy in relation to patient care, and they are described below. Although changes have occurred through technological advances and the expansion of practice areas, the functions listed here remain pertinent:

1. To create opportunities for psychiatric patients to develop more satisfying relationships, to assist them in releasing or sublimating emotional drives, and to use as a diagnostic tool
2. To help increase or restore physical function to joints and improve muscle strength and coordination
3. To help patients perform activities of daily living—eating, dressing, and so forth— and successfully use adaptive equipment and prostheses
4. To help patients readjust to home routines through the adaptation of household equipment and work simplification
5. To help patients develop and maintain special skills as required by their jobs
6. To assess the patient's physical and mental capacities, degree of social adjustment, interests, work habits, skills, and potential employability
7. To help the patient accept and make optimal use of periods of hospitalization and convalescence
8. To help patients reassess leisure and work interests

Occupational therapists are concerned with the components of performance needed to maintain self-care, work, and play or leisure activities. These components include:

- **Motor functioning.** Range of motion, muscle strength, tone, functional use, gross and fine motor skills
- **Sensory integrative functioning.** Body integration, body scheme, posture, visual-spatial awareness, sensorimotor integration, reflex and sensory development
- **Cognitive functioning.** Verbal and written communication, concentration, problem solving, time management, conceptualization, integration of learning
- **Psychological functioning.** Emotional states and feelings, coping behaviors, defense mechanisms, self-identity, self-concept
- **Social functioning.** One-to-one or group interactions

The client population served by occupational therapy is representative of the total life span from infancy through old age. Occupational therapy serves those whose abilities to cope with the tasks of daily living are impaired by environmental deprivation; developmental defect; physical, emotional, or social trauma; illness; or the life demands and changes reflected in the aging process.

These services are primarily located in rehabilitation facilities, acute or chronic care hospitals, nursing homes, community agencies, children's schools, treatment centers, developmental institutions, senior citizens' centers, private homes, and private practice facilities. Other locations are diverse and may include research centers, industry, psychiatric centers, juvenile detention centers or prisons, camps for handicapped individuals, federal and state health agencies, and so forth. Occupational therapists may choose to work exclusively with children or adolescents, with only adults, or with a combination of children and adults, depending on the setting selected for employment.

The tasks necessary to productive life at each age level are the treatment tools of the therapist: the activities used by the child to learn and grow through play; the socialization activities of adolescence; the homemaking, child-rearing, and work-related activities of the adult; and the self-help skills that serve the individual throughout life, such as eating, dressing, personal hygiene, and communications.

The occupational therapist works collaboratively with members of other health-related professions and is an integral member of the professional team. Although members of the team vary in relation to the individual client's problem, they may include qualified physicians, nurses, physical therapists, speech pathologists, social workers, psychologists, rehabilitation counselors, therapeutic recreation specialists, teachers, chaplains, counselors, and others. Specialists involved as needed might be artificial limb makers (prosthetists) and brace makers (orthotists).

The patient or client and his or her family are important members of the decision-making process regarding the management of the problem. The occupational therapist in many instances serves as an advisor in assisting the patient-family group in making decisions and in carrying out home-prescribed routines, such as exercises, follow-up management, and self-care procedures.

Within the medical framework, the ultimate responsibility for the patient rests with the physician in charge. The physician seeks information from others on which to base decisions, but it is he or she who prescribes medication, surgery, and the rehabilitation therapies that include occupational therapy. The referral of an individual to the occupational therapist requires that an evaluation be made of ability and loss of ability and that a performance treatment plan be formulated.

In a community setting, a therapist may function as an extension of a medical institution and will work under the above referral system. In other cases, the therapist may work in a health-related rather than a medical institution, such as a child care or senior citizen center. In these cases, an occupational therapist may be working without a physician's referral. Here the treatment program will be planned in relation to the goals of the institution, the needs of the individual patient or client, and in collaboration with the personnel of the agency.

In an educational setting, the therapist works collaboratively with the teaching staff and other health-care personnel to establish goals for each individual through the team process. Treatment programs in schools focus on needs of the children with respect to education-related benefits.

Teamwork

A rehabilitation team is multidisciplinary, with each member contributing specialized educational background and expertise. This sharing of different viewpoints leads to more comprehensive problem solving with regard to the patient or client, who is also considered a vital member of the team whenever possible. Family members may also play an important role in the team process.

As indicated, a wide variety of professionals work together to offer the most effective aid to help people mobilize their own resources. All team members are concerned with the welfare of the patient or client. It is important for the occupational therapist to coordinate efforts with all of the personnel who are working toward the rehabilitation of each patient or client. This is the total rehabilitation team. The number and types of professional services vary considerably according to each individual's overall needs.

It is most important that the rehabilitation team members work effectively together. This is accomplished through staff meetings, circulated reports, and other collaborative efforts.

The Physician

In a medical or institutional setting, the patient's physician, regardless of specialty, becomes the coordinator of the treatment process. The physician may be a neurologist, orthopedist, surgeon, internist, physiatrist (a doctor of physical medicine), pediatrician, or a practitioner of other medical specialties.

The Nurse

The hospital nurse is responsible for the patient's care twenty-four hours a day. He or she must see to the patient's bodily care and comfort, meals, medication, and appointments with other departments, such as x-ray, surgery, laboratory, and physical and occupational therapy. In addition, the nurse often is the person in charge of the unit and is kept informed regarding the patients. No patient ever should leave or be taken from the ward without the knowledge of the nurse in charge of that patient's care.

The Social Worker

The social worker can be the professional liaison between the patient, the family, and the physician or other health-care worker. Through interviewing, the social worker obtains a history that includes pertinent information needed to understand the patient's particular situation. For example, educational level, family and community relationships, religious beliefs and attitudes, home situation, and employment history might be of importance. Financial status determines whether financial assistance should be sought. The social worker arranges financial assistance if necessary.

In some settings (for example, counseling centers, drug and alcohol abuse treatment centers, and some psychiatric treatment facilities) social workers may conduct extensive individual and group counseling. In almost all inpatient or residential facilities, social workers help in planning the transition from the facility to the community or the transfer to another facility.

The Physical Therapist

The physical therapist evaluates and treats movement dysfunctions of anatomic or physiologic origin to maximize health and function. Problems in the musculoskeletal, neurological, cardiovascular, and pulmonary systems are treated, and individual therapists often have specialized areas of competence that influence their caseloads. Exercise, massage, ambulation training, and other techniques may be used to accomplish goals. Modalities including hydrotherapy and ultrasound, and diathermy also might be used during specific treatment programs.

As with all of the health professions, some physical therapists engage in research, consultation, or education. Physical therapy assistants work under the direct supervision of a physical therapist to help carry out treatment programs.

The Vocational Counselor

The team includes a vocational counselor when there is a need to plan a new vocational objective for the patient or client. The counselor accumulates information regarding capabilities, limitations, aptitudes, interests, and skills. Information is provided by the counselor concerning the various vocations that are possible despite the disability. Once a vocational objective is reached, plans are made for any necessary training, the patient is assisted in finding employment, and follow-up is carried out to determine work adjustment.

The Psychologist

The psychologist usually has two broad functions: aiding the patient in adjustment and collecting diagnostic information. He or she helps to alleviate emotional problems that do not require medication. The psychologist obtains diagnostic information by testing intelligence, interests, aptitudes, and personality. These tests yield information that is helpful to other professionals treating the individual. In the event that there is no vocational counselor on the staff, the psychologist may assume these responsibilities.

The Speech-Language Pathologist

The speech-language pathologist evaluates individuals with dysfunctional language or speech and provides treatment for such problems. Some speech-language clinicians also evaluate and treat difficulties associated with eating that involve the musculature of the mouth and swallowing.

The Therapeutic Recreation Specialist

The therapeutic recreation specialist plans for the recreational needs of patients. Programs may be entirely group oriented or they may be developed according to the needs of each member of the group. The most common goal is to find a combination of these two approaches. Recreation plans may include movies, dances, outings, concerts, special holiday events, opportunities for religious worship, sports, games, and music programs. Programs include both active and passive participation.

Working Together

All therapeutic programming must be carefully coordinated and must work toward the same objectives for the patient or client, and this requires extensive planning and scheduling.

The occupational therapist, therefore, must plan in terms of the total program of several or many other disciplines. No single professional can do a complete job of rehabilitation, as each has a proper place and must recognize the contributions of other disciplines. Total health care requires that all disciplines work together to promote the patient's return to the community.

2

Development of the Occupational Therapy Field

The profession of occupational therapy has its roots in the development of psychiatry and in the philosophy of treatment of the mentally ill. Several centuries ago, patients with mental disturbances were not understood to be ill but were thought to be under a spell or possessed by demons. In many instances, these individuals were beaten, put in chains, and imprisoned in cells or left to die.

It was not until the eighteenth century that the progressive thinking of a few doctors in Spain, France, England, Germany, and later in the United States, removed these sick people from their imprisonment and isolation and put them to work. They were assigned to various tasks concerned with the maintenance of the institution. In addition, diversions such as musical concerts, lectures, rides through the countryside, and so forth, were provided, and classes were designed to give instruction in educational subjects and in manual activities.

To the surprise of all concerned, many patients who were assigned to diverse activity programs not only got well faster, they often recovered completely. There are numerous fascinating records concerned with the growing recognition of the therapeutic values of activity therapy during the latter part of the eighteenth and throughout the nineteenth centuries.

Occupations used as treatment for mentally ill patients began a new concept of health care that spread rapidly in Western Europe and the United States. In the early 1800s, aides were used in carrying out this new concept in the management of mentally ill patients in the various hospital industries, such as farming, dairy work, laundry, clerical work, and housekeeping. Eventually teachers and instructors were employed in the hospitals that utilized work programs of this kind, but these personnel lacked a background in psychology and medicine. Dr. Herbert Hall was among the first to recognize this need in the early twentieth century. He employed highly skilled instructors in the arts and crafts and taught them about anatomy, physiology, and psychology. He also began the systematic use of occupations for treatment by developing a series of progressive steps to serve the physical and/or mental needs of his patients. In 1906 a nurse in Boston, Susan Tracy, gave a course to nurses in "Invalid Occupations." Several similar courses followed in different parts of the United States. This was the beginning of an organized approach toward the education of those involved in the care of the mentally ill.

As early as 1912, this claim was advanced in an article published in Germany:

> As a physician, it is my prerogative to draw emphatic attention
> to the not yet sufficiently appreciated advantages of occupations
> for the afflicted, both mental and physical. The close intervening

of the psychic functions with the somatic processes makes medical treatment without sufficient consideration of both aspects unthinkable.

Today, this consideration of both psychic functions and somatic processes underlies the basic philosophy of occupational therapy.

A Young Profession: 1917–44

In 1917 a small group of people met and formed an association, originally called the National Society for the Promotion of Occupational Therapy and later incorporated as the American Occupational Therapy Association (AOTA). George Edward Barton, a founding member, was responsible for originating the term *occupational therapy*, and Dr. H. A. Pattison presented the infant organization with this first official definition: "Occupational therapy may be defined as any activity, mental or physical, definitely prescribed for the distinct purpose of contributing to and hastening recovery from disease or injury."

World War I

With the entrance of the United States into World War I in 1917, the surgeon general of the U.S. Army requested occupational therapists for overseas service and ordered the establishment of three-month training courses to train these "reconstruction aides." Following World War I, doctors who had used this form of treatment with war-injured patients overseas requested its use in civilian hospitals. Thus occupational therapy began to emerge as a definite professional adjunct to medicine in the management of a variety of disabilities, including both mental and physical disabilities.

The Establishment of Standards

Minimum standards for the training of occupational therapists were developed in 1922 and at first were based on three-month courses that were established in Boston, Philadelphia, and St. Louis. Courses were expanded until the 1940s, when all programs were established in four-year colleges and universities within the framework of baccalaureate degree programs. In 1935 the American Medical Association undertook the evaluation and approval of educational programs in occupational therapy. This has been a joint process with the American Occupational Therapy Association.

In 1936, to protect patients and therapists, the American Occupational Therapy Association established a registration procedure for qualified therapists. This led to the development of standards for practice and the assessment of individuals to meet those standards. Certification by successful completion of a national examination was established in 1946. Organizational changes in 1986 led to the formation of the American Occupational Therapy Certification Board, which now issues the certificates.

World War II

When mobilization for a second world war began, the occupational therapy profession was ill prepared to meet the urgent personnel demands that were to be made. There were approximately nine hundred registered therapists in the country to be divided between civilian hospitals and those of the armed forces. Many new schools were developed, shortened war emergency courses were organized, and a large volunteer corps was trained. Working with those who were injured in war expanded the knowledge and skill of therapists who worked with severely handicapped patients. This was a period of specialization, when therapists developed skills in working with various orthopedic, neurological, and other injuries and first became involved in making orthotic devices, such as assistive splints.

Expansion and Consolidation: 1945–64

Following World War II, expansion continued with emphasis on rehabilitation of the chronic diseases of an aging population, such as arthritis, cancer, heart disease, stroke, and other diseases of the nervous system. A new philosophy was developing as the process of the multidisciplinary team approach to treatment was recognized as essential to quality patient care. During this period, therapists also began practicing in the public school system.

This new approach was greatly aided by the impetus of state and federal legislation that supported the development of health programs by funding the construction of rehabilitation facilities and traineeships for students in education.

Standards for occupational therapy education were strengthened when the American Occupational Therapy Association undertook an intensive three-year curriculum analysis. This study was directed toward the following:

- Job analysis of the profession
- Curriculum analysis of the educational programs
- Matching the instructional patterns against job demands to determine the functional status of curricula

The results led to many educational actions and changes, such as holding annual workshops for educators and the development of behavioral objectives for educational programs. Another outgrowth of this project was the plan to initiate entry-level programs at the master's level for students who had completed baccalaureates in other fields.

The World Federation of Occupational Therapists was founded in 1952, when representatives from ten national organizations, including the American Occupational Therapy Association, met and drew up bylaws and educational standards for all member countries. Seven years later, the World Federation of Occupational Therapists affiliated as a nongovernmental organization with the World Health Organization, which is dedicated to promoting high standards of health throughout the world. (See also Chapter 9.)

The young profession continued to be plagued by personnel shortages due to a lack of sufficient schools to educate the number of therapists needed. Another factor that kept the numbers of practicing therapists down was the attrition rate to marriage and raising a family, since the profession had historically been dominated by women. During the 1940s, men began entering the field in increasing numbers.

In an effort to extend these limited personnel resources, in 1958 the AOTA endorsed the education of occupational therapy assistants. Once again educational standards were established and a system for accrediting schools and for certifying graduates was planned. This has been a highly successful undertaking, and certified occupational therapy assistants are making valuable contributions to patient and educational programs.

In 1964 the AOTA authorized the formation of a foundation. The American Occupational Therapy Foundation is organized exclusively for charitable scientific, literary, and educational purposes. The foundation has provided scholarships and fellowships; supported special studies, surveys, and research; and published monographs, visual aids, and special reports.

Continued Growth: 1965–87

Phenomenal growth has occurred in occupational therapy during the past forty years. Thousands of new therapists enter the field each year, and still the demand for services grows. New areas of need calling for the skills and theoretical knowledge of occupational therapists continue to emerge. As quality health care has become increasingly available to more of the population, expansion has occurred in traditional areas and new service delivery systems have developed.

In the 1960s, community mental health centers came into existence to treat the emotionally ill in their home communities rather than at a few large state or private institutions. In the same decade, Medicare became a reality, providing a federally sponsored health-insurance program for the elderly. Medicaid also was developed as a federally sponsored, state-administered program for those with low incomes. Occupational therapists were needed along with other health professionals to provide services for people covered under these plans.

In the 1970s, Public Law 94-142, mandating education for all handicapped children, caused public schools to hire large numbers of related services personnel, including occupational therapists, to meet the needs of children with all types of disabling conditions.

The 1970s also saw astounding growth in medical knowledge, and relevant new information was used by occupational therapists to improve their treatment methods. Many new health-related businesses sprang up to provide equipment and supplies for diagnosis and treatment. Occupational therapists benefited from the manufacture of adapted equipment that once had to be made by hand (examples include eating aids, wheelchair adaptations, and therapy equipment of all types). Splints of certain kinds became available in graduated sizes and in improved materials, thus relieving occupational therapists of the need to design and cut every splint individually.

With the increase in the number of therapists and the variety of specialty areas in which occupational therapists work, a need for greater sharing of information became evident. Professional groups made up of therapists from a number of occupational therapy specialty areas initiated newsletters for members and began holding meetings at the state and national levels to share issues, concerns, and up-to-date information. A national student association also developed, giving students a combined voice and a means of sharing and growing in their chosen profession.

The increase in the number of therapists and the growing trend toward obtaining master's and doctoral degrees led to a proliferation of new books and journals. These factors added impetus to the study of the profession's philosophical bases. Research became more important as therapists sought to validate theory and practice. With more therapists obtaining postbaccalaureate degrees, research skills began to be used more in clinical situations. Skills in research methods are of great practical value in studying the effects of treatment to ensure quality of care.

State licensing of occupational therapists has increased so that almost all fifty states, the District of Columbia, and Puerto Rico now have such laws in place. These laws protect both the public and therapists.

Diversity and Growth: 1988–Present

According to the U.S. Bureau of Labor Statistics, occupational therapists held about eighty-two thousand jobs in 2002, and a 45 percent increase in job openings is projected by 2012. Clearly it is a growing and dynamic field.

The expansion of the profession and the resultant greater visibility of its practitioners, along with efforts by the American Occupational Therapy Association and state associations to educate the public about occupational therapy, have created increased demand for services and a tremendous increase in the number of students seeking admission to academic programs. Many colleges and universities have added programs, with occupational therapy now being offered at more than two hundred colleges and universities in the United States, including the District of Columbia and Puerto Rico.

Growth has brought diversity. Occupational therapists have a wide variety of job choices with excellent salaries and benefits. Salaries for occupational therapists and occupational therapy assistants have risen substantially over the years. (See Chapter 9 for information about salary levels.)

Interest in specialization and in gaining recognition for expertise in various practice areas or treatment techniques appears to have increased. For example, therapists might seek pediatric certification or certified hand therapist status or certification in neurodevelopmental therapy. More than half of the registered therapists surveyed in the past ten years considered themselves to be specialists rather than generalists, whether or not they had any specialty certification. Therapists often assume a primary role in a treatment area and therefore "specialize" in it. In addition, approximately one-third of registered occupational therapists and almost one-quarter of certified occupational therapy assistants consider consultation their secondary employment function.

As one reflects on the history of occupational therapy, it can be seen that amazing growth has occurred in the relatively short existence of the profession. The years ahead are expected to bring additional quality changes.

Future of the Profession

What does the future hold for the profession of occupational therapy in terms of practice? The American Occupational Therapy Association interviewed leaders in the profession to obtain their perspective. Some believe that occupational therapists will work in increasingly diverse settings in both medical and nonmedical areas, including ergonomics, driver rehabilitation and training, welfare-to-work services, and health and wellness consulting. The greater life expectancy of Americans will increase the need for therapists working with the elderly, and the greater awareness among parents of disabled children of the services available will increase the demand for pediatric occupational therapists working in hospitals, schools, homes, and nursing homes.

The U.S. Bureau of Labor Statistics projects that the demand for occupational therapists should continue to rise as a result of growth in the number of individuals with disabilities or limited function who require therapy services. The baby-boom generation's movement into middle age, a period when the incidence of heart attack and stroke increases, will spur the demand for therapeutic services. Growth in the population seventy-five years and older, an age group that suffers from high incidences of disabling conditions, also will increase the demand for therapeutic services. In addition, medical advances now enable more patients with critical problems to survive, and these patients ultimately may need extensive therapy.

Hospitals will continue to employ a large number of occupational therapists to provide therapy services to acutely ill inpatients.

Hospitals also will need occupational therapists to staff their out-patient rehabilitation programs.

Employment growth in schools will result from the expansion of the school-age population and extended services for disabled students. Therapists will be needed to help children with disabilities prepare to enter special education programs.

Rehabilitation is effective in returning workers to their jobs after injury sooner and in better physical condition than without skilled intervention, and employers and insurers will no doubt value the cost-effectiveness of such services and increasingly make use of them. In the area of mental health, the American Occupational Therapy Association will promote therapist interest and practice in this once primary area of occupational therapy.

There will be a need in the profession for scholars and clinician researchers who can provide the research base that is necessary for practice. New treatments developed from theory will evolve, and current treatments will remain or be eliminated based on their effectiveness, as proven or disproven through research.

Despite all the anticipated changes, an emphasis on function is expected to remain as a core concept in occupational therapy. Occupational therapists will continue to work to improve performance deficits.

Ethical practice will also be addressed more closely in the health professions, just as it is being addressed in business, government, and other areas of our society. Occupational therapists will be encouraged to take an active role in related organizations at the local, state, national, and international levels so that they may be advocates for both the profession and for those who use its services. Occupational therapists will need to be aware of how the delivery of their services fits within the total system of which it is a part, including the total health-care system and systems specific to each practice setting.

Rapid changes are occurring in the health-care system, and the future under any anticipated national health-care reform cannot be accurately predicted. If the goal of improved access to health care, including occupational therapy services, is reached, then the need for therapists may expand even more than presently predicted.

Health Care and Prevention

The past several years have witnessed the emergence of new emphases and thrusts in the area of health-care delivery. Occupational therapy had previously functioned largely within the medical model of patient care, with primary emphasis on treatment and recovery following illness or injury. This emphasis is still strong, but other philosophies of health-care delivery are emerging.

Health, rather than *illness*, has now become the key word, and efforts are being directed toward the prevention of dysfunction and the maintenance of function. Thus the community model of health-care delivery has been established, with services frequently offered in patient homes and in community centers rather than in hospitals. Services are needed in mental health crisis centers, senior citizen facilities, halfway houses, outpatient rehabilitation departments, nursery schools, educational institutions, and in the public school systems.

In the area of patient care, much attention is now directed toward the early identification of learning and developmental problems requiring sensory, cognitive, motor, and social stimulation through various techniques of occupational therapy. Care of the aging in community centers, nursing homes, and continued-care facilities has become a major area of specialization.

The need to evaluate the efficiency of both clinical and educational programs has led to increasing research. As questions are identified, an organized methodology is being employed in the search for answers.

Occupational therapy is responding to changing societal needs and to rapid advances in health-care technology. Members of the profession are contributing to the knowledge explosion in unique, creative, and beneficial ways.

The years from 1917 to the present have witnessed the maturation of an idea and philosophy into a fully developed profession. This is a proud heritage of hard work and accomplishment. Occupational therapy provides a service to society. The profession has a unique body of knowledge increasingly documented by research and established standards of practice as well as a code of ethics. A strong national association allows for leadership and direction.

3

THE OCCUPATIONAL
THERAPY PROCESS

OCCUPATIONAL THERAPISTS WORK with individuals who have conditions that are mentally, physically, developmentally, or emotionally disabling. They help patients develop, recover, or maintain daily living and work skills. The goal of occupational therapists is to help their clients have independent, satisfying, and productive lives.

These clients often seek occupational therapy services on their own, or physicians or other professionals may refer them for services. The need for a physician's referral is apparent in medical settings. The logical sequence of steps in determining and meeting patient or client needs is called the *occupational therapy process*. It consists of screening, evaluation, treatment planning, treatment implementation, and reevaluation. Throughout the process, the occupational therapist must exercise careful thought and problem-solving skills.

Screening

In the screening phase, the occupational therapist customarily determines important information about the patient's or client's condition. Access to records of any prior or current health care, an interview with the individual, and brief screening tests are some of the methods employed in learning about the status and potential for benefit from available services. The screening part of the process is a general stage rather than a specific detail-finding stage. Major areas investigated might include a rough estimate of developmental level (particularly in a child or developmentally disabled adult), ability to carry out daily living skills or work responsibilities, and ability to engage in meaningful leisure activities.

The occupational therapist attempts to determine specific areas that will require further evaluation and, if possible, to estimate length of treatment required. Records of findings and interpretations must be kept for documentation purposes. Recommendations are made for further action or referral based on available services. It may be necessary to consult with a team social worker or with other health professionals and agencies to seek help if there is a lack of financial resources for necessary care.

The certified occupational therapy assistant (COTA), supervised by a registered occupational therapist (OTR), may assist in the screening process by performing such necessary tasks as obtaining data from medical charts, interviewing relatives, and carrying out some measurements.

Evaluation

Evaluation involves in-depth gathering of data in the specific areas needed for planning and implementing treatment. The therapist attempts to find the reasons for any deficiencies in a patient's ability to function in the life areas of self-care, work, and play or leisure activities. Factors interfering with life functioning can be physical, cognitive, emotional, or social in nature, and it is the task of the occupational therapist to investigate problem areas carefully so that he or she can implement effective treatment that will help the patient or client return to satisfying, productive, and maximally independent living.

The methods that are used in evaluation include some of those that are used during screening, but they are more thoroughly utilized, and other investigative means can be employed as well. In addition to interviewing and reading records for information about the patient's previous medical, social, and employment history, formal tests and measurements and structured observations may be used. Specific areas evaluated will depend on the individual patient's or client's problem areas and the particular therapist's area of practice. Some areas that are commonly evaluated include musculoskeletal status, sensory integration capabilities, physical or psychological daily living skills, cognition, psychological (emotional) status, social or interpersonal relationships, and potential for return to work.

Any data that are gathered must be documented and interpreted, and often a formal report is sent to the referring source. The report usually takes into consideration the individual's abilities and disabilities—both physical and emotional—his or her interpersonal support systems, and his or her personal motivation toward independence. As mentioned earlier, the certified occupational therapy assistant, under the supervision of a registered occupational therapist, may be involved in some areas of the evaluation, such as assessing daily living skills, testing for joint range of motion and muscle strength, and determining wheelchair mobility status.

Treatment Plan

In the treatment planning phase, the registered occupational therapist uses evaluation results to formulate prioritized goals and develop treatment objectives that specify means for achieving goals in step-by-step fashion. When possible, the therapist works with the patient or client to set goals of personal value to the individual. The objectives identify the approach, methods, techniques, and media to be used. The certified occupational therapy assistant is an integral part of this process, since in many areas he or she may be guiding the patient or client through treatment.

The treatment plan is fulfilled by using tasks and treatment methods involving as much active participation of the patient or client as possible. Treatment is designed to bring about the desired improvements and reach goals set in physical, developmental, emotional, social, or cognitive areas. The OTR and COTA have been trained to analyze activities for their component parts and their possible value in achieving goals. For example, an activity can be analyzed for the specific movements and muscle use involved, for the types of cognitive processes required, for the stimulating or sedating nature of the task, for the interpersonal reactions that might be elicited, and so forth.

Implementation of Treatment

In implementing the treatment plan, occupational therapists may use many means to help the patient or client reach the established goals. They use verbal means to guide and teach, encourage, motivate, and provide feedback regarding general behavior or specific performance. They must think creatively to solve clients' problems and lead them to triumph over mental or physical disabilities.

The use of activities in treatment allows the patient or client to be involved in his or her own habilitation or rehabilitation in a participatory way. Active involvement in purposeful activities to fulfill goals is believed to be the primary way by which human beings learn, change, and attain life satisfaction. Activities may be used with individuals and with groups. Work, play, sports, games, crafts, exercise through task participation, food preparation, computer use, and many other life activities may be used to meet specific goals of a physical, psychological, or developmental nature.

At times preliminary splinting, neuromuscular facilitation techniques, or exercise with or without equipment may be used before a physically disabled individual can participate to any extent in life activities. The main goal of all treatment in occupational therapy is to achieve as much independence as possible. Developing strength, endurance, range of motion, and coordination are also goals.

In some cases, items must be adapted to allow a person more independence and greater comfort. Sometimes a simple attachment to a commonly used item (such as a spoon, hairbrush, or pencil) will make it usable, while other adaptations may be quite complex. Therapists may work with rehabilitation engineers to design equipment. Communication and learning may be enhanced through adapting computers and typewriters. Techniques of body use to maximize strength and mobility may free a person from dependence on others for dressing, transferring from bed to wheelchair, and so on. A client may be taught work simplification techniques to conserve energy. Adaptations along with training may allow greater personal freedom, as with special wheelchairs or through automobile training with the use of hand controls or other adaptations that permit driving despite a physical disability.

Assertiveness training or stress management techniques may lead a client to have a sense of well being and greater control over his or her life; a group activity in which everyone must work together and interrelate well enough to accomplish the designated task affords an excellent opportunity for an individual not only to gain insight into his or her behavior, but also to use such a setting as a laboratory for attempting new behaviors. Field trips out of a facility may be used to encourage reentry into the community by providing opportunities for head-injured or long-term mentally ill persons to relearn the skills that are needed for taking public transportation, buying grocery items, and learning to carry out a sequence of steps in everyday tasks.

As can be seen from the above descriptions, occupational therapy treatment might take many forms, including many not mentioned here. For a person who likes challenge and reward in making other people's lives better, occupational therapy is an excellent career choice.

Reevaluation

Reevaluation at intervals during the course of treatment helps the therapist determine progress and ensure effective, quality care. Results might indicate either that the current treatment is producing the desired changes or that an alternative treatment plan should be developed. It also might indicate that maximum benefits have been achieved and that treatment may be discontinued. Maximum benefits may not necessarily mean that the individual has achieved full function but only that further treatment is unwarranted at the present time. When treatment is discontinued, the therapist must make certain that arrangements are made for any necessary follow-up care or referrals.

Treatment Areas

Occupational therapy intervention is directed toward the alleviation of actual or potential loss of function in one or more spheres of life: physical, emotional, social, and vocational. In the following discussion of treatment areas, try to visualize how the separate areas combine and overlap to form a unique treatment program for each patient or client.

Physical Dysfunction

Many diseases affect muscles so that they do not act reciprocally as they should; these muscles are referred to as *uncoordinated.* Exercises are given to improve coordination and enable the patient to perform motions correctly and smoothly. Techniques for applying sensory stimulation to skin, muscles, and joints (for example, stroking, tapping, pressure, or joint movement) may be used to encourage improved voluntary movement and task performance.

Some patients who will never again use a paralyzed arm or leg must, nevertheless, be taught to care for themselves. They must learn how to use perhaps only two extremities (limbs), and to use their residual abilities in spite of their handicaps. When full restoration or correction of a patient's physical problems is impossible, the occupational therapist may teach compensation techniques.

The occupational therapist also works with patients who have undergone amputation and must learn to use an artificial leg or arm. In this situation, the therapist employs a range of daily living techniques and teaches the patient how to work with the prosthesis. The ability to use a prosthesis encourages greater independence in the patient.

For some patients, the therapist utilizes procedures that will increase the circulation of blood to the injured area, for this in itself may hasten the healing process.

The occupational therapist works with children and adults with cerebral palsy and contributes a great deal in this field. These are neurologically impaired individuals who may have defects of motor control and speech, hearing, or visual problems. Physical habilitation is carried out through neuromuscular techniques, traditional exercise, and daily living skills training. Adaptive devices for self-care, communication, and play are selected or designed to meet individual needs. For example, one child might need adapted utensils for feeding himself or herself or a computer adaptation for learning, communication, and fun. When working with handicapped children, a therapist must never forget that they are children first and that they have children's psychological and social needs.

Children with cerebral palsy and other disabling conditions must be provided experiences that give them the sensory input they do not receive through most children's customary play activities. They also must be given as many skills as possible to make their lives less frustrating and more independent and satisfying.

Regardless of the diagnosis, emotional reactions of the patient are inevitable. Whether the occupational therapist is treating a person with an orthopedic problem, a heart condition, or a spinal cord injury, the therapist is treating the patient as a total person and considers psychological needs and responses in addition to the physical problems. A well-planned occupational therapy program can prevent problems before they arise, as well as alleviate any problems that may develop.

Psychosocial Dysfunction

Therapists working in psychiatric settings may work with patients exhibiting psychotic behaviors as a result of illnesses such as schizophrenia, bipolar disorder (manic-depressive psychosis), or paranoia. In those settings and in community-based facilities serving less severely disturbed individuals, occupational therapists may work with persons demonstrating anxiety, drug and alcohol problems, dysthymic disorders (neuroses), disturbances caused by transient life situations, and other conditions.

Occupational therapists also may work to promote mental health in wellness programs, providing guidance to alleviate stress, increase coping skills, improve self-concept, and so forth. Guidance to improve skills for successful interpersonal relationships may help patients or clients become more comfortable with themselves. It will also help them be more satisfied with their lives. Activities are carefully chosen to develop and enhance successful behaviors.

Occupational therapy for the emotionally ill may be directed toward the following goals:

- To reinforce mental health through teaching the patient, family, or other caregivers to structure the environment in which the patient lives and works
- To evaluate a patient's ability and willingness to relate to other people
- To plan and carry out treatment programs designed to influence the emotional disorder in a positive way
- To contribute to the social and vocational adjustment of the patient in his or her community

To do this, the therapist must have an understanding of the meaning of behavior and of the dynamics of human relationships. It is a goal of occupational therapists working in psychiatric facilities to provide a therapeutic environment that will aid recovery. With this understanding, the occupational therapist is able to plan specific therapy programs designed to encourage independent living, vocational readiness, and social competence.

Social Objectives

Socially, the therapist has a valuable contribution to make to humankind, for each person is basically a social being. The skills of occupational therapy have a significant social meaning.

The patient is encouraged to participate in social activity, to see herself or himself as a contributing member of the group rather than as one set apart. The patient is aided to realize her or his abilities in meeting the demands of the social order.

More generally, the therapist has a responsibility to the community at large. One of the social objectives of occupational therapy is to assist the patient in coping with disability and to understand his or her potential despite that disability. This state of social readiness, of returning to an active community role, is fostered by the occupational therapist.

Vocational Evaluation

Prevocational exploration and vocational evaluation have achieved a prominent place in the total rehabilitation of the patient. By definition, prevocational exploration implies an early screening and evaluation process to ascertain the patient's work tolerance, physical strength, and ability to meet the demands of the work situation.

This prevocational exploration of basic work skills, work habits, motivation, and interests is recorded on evaluation record forms. The occupational therapist then acts as an evaluator of the general skills of the patient or client and of his or her specific vocational skills.

The therapist also assists with special problems of work adaptation, interpreting performance difficulties to work supervisors and providing the supportive link between medical rehabilitation and job placement.

The rehabilitation process must be oriented to the total needs of the patient, whether medical, psychological, social, or vocational. Even in a strictly medical setting there is the need for initial vocational planning. In some occupational therapy skill activities, careful observation of the patient or client can give important job-related information regarding work habits, temperament, emotional stability, interests, and manual dexterity.

Essentially, the vocational evaluation process consists of skills analysis, activity observation, physical capacities evaluation, and exploration of work potential through job samples and aptitude tests. This process is followed by the occupational therapist's recommendations and a final report of findings to the vocational counselor and any referring physician or agency. Vocational training and actual job placement are usually handled by persons with industrial experience and placement training.

Economic Factors

Economically, therapists have a part to play in hastening recovery of patients, thereby decreasing lost work time. Many occupational therapists in hospitals, rehabilitation facilities, and private practice incorporate work programs and functional capacities evaluations into their programs. Some provide consultation to business and industry representatives regarding methods of preventing consistently recurring injuries that result from repetitive or overly stressful physical tasks.

Today a number of insurance companies refer industrial accident cases to rehabilitation units for treatment, including both occupational and physical therapy. The time saved in recovery, and, therefore, in compensation, far outweighs the expense of treatment.

4

ENTERING THE PROFESSION

THIS CHAPTER WILL detail the requirements needed to enter the field of occupational therapy at the professional and assistant levels. Both qualifications (for occupational therapist and occupational therapy assistant) have the following entry-level requirements:

1. Educational preparation leading to qualification by the American Occupational Therapy Association
2. Personal qualifications including individual characteristics, interests, and attributes
3. Good physical and emotional health

Education

Education includes an understanding of life tasks and skills, interpersonal relationships, social roles, and human functions. The educational foundation needed by the student should be developed through a strong background of college preparatory work in high school and should continue with liberal arts and science courses in college. Courses may include English composition, literature and speech, biological science, natural sciences, psychology, sociology, history, foreign language, art, and mathematics.

You can enhance your educational experience by participating in extracurricular activities; this will help you develop hobbies and interests through which you will meet many different kinds of people. A successful occupational therapist should enjoy being with people and should be sensitive to and have an appreciation for the needs of others. Your communication skills—written and oral as well as nonverbal—are very important. You need problem-solving and decision-making skills, and you must be able to analyze and interpret situations and various data. Only as much as you understand yourself—your strengths and weaknesses and your philosophy of life—can you be helpful to others in regaining lost patterns of behavior. Students currently in occupational therapy educational programs recommend gaining firsthand experience of occupational therapy through visiting clinical programs and volunteering or working as occupational therapy aides.

Registered Occupational Therapist

Currently a bachelor's degree in occupational therapy is the minimum requirement to enter this field. Beginning in 2007, however, a master's degree or higher will be the minimum educational requirement. All states, the District of Columbia, and Puerto Rico regulate the practice of occupational therapy; many jurisdictions mandate periodic continuing education requirements. To obtain a license, applicants must graduate from an accredited educational program and pass a national certification examination. Those who pass are awarded the title Registered Occupational Therapist (OTR).

The occupational therapist completes an entry-level master's or entry-level doctoral degree at one of more than three hundred accredited programs at colleges and universities throughout the United States. (See Appendix A for accredited programs.) Occupational therapy students must also complete a six-month supervised fieldwork program and pass a national certification exam.

Occupational therapy course work includes physical, biological, and behavioral sciences and the application of occupational therapy theory and skills.

Admission Requirements

Specific admission requirements are established by the individual colleges and universities. As soon as you have determined a career plan and identified potential colleges or universities, it is important to learn the admission requirements that you must be prepared to meet at the school of your choice.

If you are a high school student planning a career in occupational therapy, the following is a list of the subjects generally required to enter college or university programs with a major in occupational therapy.

Courses
Biology, chemistry, or physics
English
History or social studies
Mathematics

A human growth and development course is required by many programs, and a basic statistics course may be required, particularly if you wish to begin an entry-level master's program. College admissions offices also look favorably at paid or volunteer experience in the health-care field.

If you are in college and want to transfer to an occupational therapy program, the following requirements have been compiled from accredited curricula in occupational therapy. Prerequisites for specific programs may be obtained by contacting the individual schools. (See Appendix A.)

Courses
Biological and/or natural sciences
English
Psychology, abnormal psychology, developmental
    psychology
Sociology or anthropology

Entry-Level Professional Education

The Accreditation Council for Occupational Therapy Education (ACOTE) of the American Occupational Therapy Association (AOTA) accredits entry-level master's and doctoral programs for the occupational therapist. All accredited programs follow the same basic outline, although variations in emphasis are found in each program, depending on the curriculum within the university or college. All programs prepare students to become competent, resourceful therapists with the necessary competencies and skills to carry out the required professional functions. The following curriculum areas and objectives serve as the basis of all educational programs.

- **Liberal arts content.** This is prerequisite to or concurrent with professional education. It will facilitate communication skills, logical thinking, critical analysis, problem solving, and creativity. Liberal arts content also is important in developing the ability to make judgments based on broad background knowledge and in developing multicultural knowledge and appreciation.

- **Biological, behavioral, and health sciences content.** A prerequisite to or concurrent with professional education, this content area encompasses normal and abnormal conditions throughout the life span. Courses include anatomy, physiology, neurosciences, and kinesiology. Other courses include content on human development and behavior; congenital, developmental, acute, and chronic disease processes and traumatic injuries, and their effect on human functioning; and effects of health and disability on individuals, families, and society.

- **Occupational therapy theory and practice content.** This includes the foundations and historical and philosophical bases of the profession and the theoretical bases and models of practice. It also includes fundamentals of activity, such as the analysis, teaching, and adapting of activities of daily living, work, and play/leisure. The occupational therapy process, based on frames of reference or theoretical perspectives, is studied in-depth, and documentation of services through appropriate record keeping also is covered.

- **Occupational therapy service management content.** This is designed to develop the ability to apply principles of management in providing services. Among other things, methods of planning, organizing, staffing, and coordinating are taught, and students learn about factors important in health-care delivery.

- **Research content.** This includes the value of research in clinical practice and professional development, components of research protocols, and interpretation and application of research study results.

• **Professional ethics content.** This is important in guiding therapists' conduct so that professional standards and ethics are respected and the profession is appropriately maintained and promoted.

• **Fieldwork education.** Fieldwork is a required component. Level I fieldwork is clinical experience obtained while students complete their course work during academic semesters. It gives students a better perspective for learning clinical applications of theories and techniques. Level II fieldwork consists of a minimum of six months of supervised full-time experience in clinical settings.

Certified Occupational Therapy Assistant

Certified occupational therapy assistants (COTA) complete an associate degree program at an accredited school. Programs are established in technical and vocational institutes, junior and community colleges, and four-year colleges. (See Appendix A.)

Admission requirements for entry into these programs include graduation from an accredited high school or the equivalent and specific course prerequisites similar to those cited earlier for the professional level.

Standards established by the American Medical Association and the American Occupational Therapy Association for assistants include the following.

• **General education.** This is prerequisite to or concurrent with technical education in that it facilitates both communication and problem-solving skills and enhances a knowledge of and appreciation for multicultural factors.

• **Biological, behavioral, and health sciences.** This is prerequisite to or concurrent with technical education in that it encompasses normal and abnormal conditions that may occur throughout the life span. Information gained in this content area includes knowledge about the human body and conditions treated in occupational therapy. Students learn about human behavior, community and environmental effects on the individual, and influences affecting health.

- **Occupational therapy principles and practice skills area.** This includes the underlying foundation, history, and philosophical bases of the profession; an emphasis on the use of purposeful activities and occupation for enhancing role function; and fundamentals of analyzing, teaching, and adapting activities of daily living, work, and play/leisure. The occupational therapy process (screening and assessment, treatment planning, implementation, reassessment, and termination) includes learning about assessment and intervention methods and collaborating with the certified occupational therapist in intervention. The occupational therapy assistant student also learns about management of services, directing activity programs, documenting services, and communicating with others. In addition, the occupational therapy assistant develops values, attitudes, and behaviors that are necessary not only to maintain the profession's standards and ethics but also to enhance the assistant's roles in the profession.

- **Fieldwork education.** There are two phases to complete in fieldwork: Level I fieldwork provides experiences that enhance classroom learning through observation and participation in basic aspects of the occupational therapy process. Level II fieldwork, for which the minimum requirement is twelve weeks of full-time experience, provides in-depth experience needed to gain entry-level competency for occupational therapy practice at the assistant level.

Some associate degree programs link into four-year baccalaureate programs, thereby enabling the assistant who is seeking career advancement to continue to the professional level without too much loss of time. A COTA desiring OTR preparation also might consider professional entry-level master's degree programs, some of which allow admission with a minimum of ninety undergraduate semester hours (equivalent to about three years of college work). These programs require sufficient credit hours at the master's level to balance out the fewer undergraduate credits.

Continuing Education

Any student entering the health professions today must recognize that education is a lifelong process. As you work with new ideas, you come to understand different dimensions of problems, ask more questions, and seek more answers.

Continuing education enables you to learn more about a specific function in a short period of time: a three-day workshop on the burned hand, a three-week refresher course in physical rehabilitation, or a one-week institute on supervision or sensory integration, for example. Many opportunities are available throughout the country; in fact, it can be difficult to decide which workshops will be most helpful at any given time. Some employers will defray the costs of one or more educational workshops per year in the interest of keeping an up-to-date treatment program, but sometimes the therapist must underwrite this expense personally.

Financial Aid and Costs

Educational costs continue to rise, and there is a great difference in expense between tax-supported institutions (state, county, or city) and privately endowed colleges. You are urged to contact the college of your choice for current information about its tuition and fees, living expenses, cost of books, and clinical fieldwork expenses.

The majority of students need to rely on financial-aid packages that may include parents' contributions, personal savings, work-study programs, educational loans, and scholarships. A student's need for financial aid is, in the simplest terms, the difference between anticipated expenses and financial resources. The determination of need will be based upon analysis of information provided by the student and/or family. Parents of dependent children ordinarily have an obligation to contribute to educational costs from discretionary income. For families below a moderate-income level, little or no family contribution can be expected, and the students will need to secure the necessary funds.

A student is considered self-supporting if he or she is an older adult who has been financially independent for some time or is not claimed as a dependent by her or his parents during a specified period preceding the determination of financial status.

If you are in need of financial assistance, you should look first to the possibilities of loans or scholarships from agencies in your community: your church, service organizations, and other local foundations. Following acceptance into an occupational therapy program, contact the financial aid officer of that institution about the sources available through the college or university. Your occupational therapy program office also may have information about the numerous hospitals or other employers that support students by paying tuition for one or two years in return for a reasonable employment commitment (usually one to two years) as a full-salaried employee upon graduation.

Sign-on bonuses, often of several thousand dollars, are given by many employers. These are not typically granted to students who receive tuition assistance from the same institution or to those who obtain the position through the services of a recruiter (because the institution must pay the recruiter for finding the therapist).

There are sources of financial aid available to you beyond your own community. The suggestions offered here are merely a starting point; a trip to your public or school library should turn up additional sources of assistance.

Federal aid is available in the form of grants and loans. Grants are outright gifts of money to help you finance your education. Your demonstrated needs plus the type of school you are attending will determine the amount of the grant.

As you no doubt expected, federal loans must eventually be repaid by the student. But the terms of repayment are very generous. You pay nothing on the loan while you are enrolled in a program. Repayment begins after you leave school, and you have up to ten years to pay off the loan at a reasonable rate of interest. Detailed information about federal financial aid is available on the Web at http://studentaid.ed.gov.

Additionally, most states have grant and scholarship funds available to their residents. Both forms of assistance are outright gifts, but scholarships are generally based on outstanding academic performance and may be renewable every year that you are in school.

Many state occupational therapy associations offer loans and scholarships to students from their states. Contact your local association for more information on these programs.

The American Occupational Therapy Foundation (AOTF) administers scholarship programs that provide financial assistance to undergraduate and graduate occupational therapy students based on need and scholastic ability. Preference is given to college juniors and seniors or to students completing occupational therapy assistant programs.

The E. K. Wise loan program assists eligible students who have baccalaureate degrees and are enrolled in advanced standing or graduate entry-level professional occupational therapy curricula, or who are enrolled in postprofessional graduate curricula in occupational therapy. The American Occupational Therapy Association provides information about financial assistance.

Certification and Licensure

After graduating from an accredited professional program for occupational therapists, the graduate is eligible to take the national certification examination, which is administered through the National Board for Certification in Occupational Therapy (NBCOT). The NBCOT offers several online exams that candidates can take at any time and from any computer with Internet access. OTR and COTA practice exams can be purchased online at www.nbcot.org. Also available at the website is a candidate handbook for those taking the tests in the United States, Canada, Puerto Rico, and Guam.

Successful completion of the certification exam leads to inclusion in a published registry of qualified professionals and the right to use the letters OTR or COTA after one's name.

Personal Attributes

In addition to meeting educational requirements, there are identifiable personal qualities that are important to all therapists.

First and foremost among these qualities is a liking for people, followed by an enjoyment in sharing oneself with others and an ease in establishing relationships. Occupational therapy is very much a people-oriented profession, involving a teaching/counseling relationship with patients or clients and a coordinating/sharing relationship with other professionals.

The therapist needs to be empathetic and perceptive to the patient's feelings at any given moment in order to determine how best to respond. The therapist must be tactful and patient in working with clients, thereby avoiding undue friction and misunderstandings. Patients are people in crisis who are worried and anxious and may understandably be short-tempered. Misunderstandings among professionals also can be energy draining and time consuming and usually result in less-effective treatment. A sense of humor is a great asset in helping to counteract the tensions of the day.

Communication skills are very important to the therapist. A good observer and listener will understand many problems before they are stated. It is also important to write and speak clearly. The therapist is a teacher with patients, families, the public, and professional colleagues; it is therefore important to be able to explain lucidly what has to be done, why it has to be done, and what results are expected.

The therapist must be prepared to write reports describing treatment programs, administrative functions, or clinical research. It may be necessary to write grant proposals to obtain funding for special projects.

The potential therapist needs a certain degree of manual dexterity in some areas of practice and enjoyment of some creative activities, such as the arts, crafts, music, drama, and dance. It is not necessary to be an expert in the creative arts, but a certain amount of familiarity with them is helpful. The basic interest of the occupational therapist should be that of the teacher/counselor who experiences pleasure in guiding others, rather than that of the creative artist whose pleasure comes from expert performance. Remember, the creativity of the therapist is centered in the patient, whereas the creativity of the artist is centered in the artistic product. Creativity helps both in the many decisions and the problem solving required in evaluating, treating, and interacting with patients, colleagues, and others.

A few experiences useful to the prospective occupational therapist are participating in special interest groups, such as music, art, drama, or journalism clubs; helping to organize social groups in school; volunteering in local hospitals and settlement houses; and leadership activities in scouting, Sunday school, summer camps for healthy or handicapped children, and community centers. Any work or travel experience is beneficial to the growth of the individual and helpful in understanding people with different interests and lifestyles.

Occupational therapy is an exacting profession that demands much of the student. The curricula can be very demanding, and good study skills, determination, and perseverance are essential. Students who must work or who have heavy home responsibilities will need good time-management skills. Foreign students must have mastery of the English language when attending school in the United States, as well as equivalent academic credentials.

The therapist must use analytical skills in identifying problems and creativity in finding solutions. This is true whether the problem involves finding the best method to treat a child, approaching a man who has just lost his sight, convincing administrators that another therapist should be employed, or setting up a research project. Patients and other personnel expect the therapist to function as a leader—a person who is well prepared to do the job, has self-confidence, uses good judgment, and is dependable and responsible. Occupational therapists should have not only the courage to express convictions but also the ability to listen to other points of view and change position when proven wrong.

Physical and Mental Requirements

If you want to help patients with physical or mental problems, you must be a well-adjusted individual. It stands to reason that you must understand yourself and your methods of responding to crises, frustration, and anxiety before you can understand and share the problems of others. If you are facing personal crises of your own, not much energy is left to give support to a sixteen-year-old boy who has just lost the use of his legs for life.

Physical health is also important because when other people are dependent on you, it is necessary to keep to your schedule. In many situations the therapist is required to do a great deal of walking through long institutional corridors or may have to travel from home to home, perhaps on public transportation and many times carrying equipment. Frequently it is necessary to support patients physically and to lift children. The therapist should ideally have acute senses of sight, hearing, and touch in order to make keen observations of the patients.

There are, however, occupational therapists with disabilities who can function well in certain settings. If you have a disability that creates a functional handicap, you will need help in evaluating whether occupational therapy is a feasible career goal for you. You should seek counsel from the school of your choice.

5

CLINICAL PRACTICE

IN THE PREVIOUS chapters we considered occupational therapy and its various functions in relation to the spectrum of professional services it renders, both on a one-to-one client basis and in its community responsibilities. In this chapter we will discuss some of the professional roles of the therapist. Broadly speaking, these roles can be divided into three large areas of rendered services:

1. **Positions in the clinical field.** In these positions, effort is directed toward patient or client treatment. These roles are at the staff and supervisory level.
2. **Positions in professional education.** These positions are concerned with curriculum, teaching, and program development at both the undergraduate and graduate levels.
3. **Positions of general administration.** These positions are found in both the educational and clinical arenas. They require accumulated experience for the coordination and

planning of various responsibilities, such as student supervision, class scheduling, curriculum structure, supervision of staff and other personnel, budget management, and personnel policies. All administrative positions are involved in planning and directing the work of others.

Research may be conducted by occupational therapists in any of the above roles or in positions designated specifically for research activities. Research is important for many reasons, including proving the value of one treatment over another.

In this chapter we will consider the job description of the clinical practitioner, who evaluates the functional potential of clients and designs programs of treatment to restore or enhance function. Administration will be dealt with more specifically in Chapter 7 and education is discussed in Chapter 8.

Specific Clinical Positions

Following are descriptions of the various clinical positions that can be held by occupational therapists.

Director of an Occupational Therapy Department

This position involves program development, implementation of planning, policy making, and all of the procedural duties for the smooth functioning of the department. In addition, the director is responsible for all personnel within the department and for all educational programs. The director reports to the medical director of the department for medical concerns and to the director of the institution or agency for administrative matters.

Assistant Department Director

The assistant department director assists the director in the organization through the administration and coordination of all of the occupational therapy units of the department. This position is usually found only in larger institutions having many separate treatment units.

Supervisor of an Occupational Therapy Unit

In an institution having several units, the supervisor of an occupational therapy unit may have both administrative and supervisory duties. The supervisor is responsible for the supervision and work assignments of staff therapists, students, auxiliary personnel, volunteers, and assistants assigned to the unit. Depending on the size of the unit, the supervisor may administer patient treatment. This person reports to the director of the department.

Supervisor of Student Fieldwork

This position entails great responsibility and preferably should be filled by a senior staff registered occupational therapist (OTR) who has experience in handling personnel and students. This administrator coordinates programs of field experience for occupational therapy students working in the department, supervising their work and keeping in close contact with the affiliating institution. Some clinical duties also may be assumed.

Job Settings

Occupational therapy offers a wide choice of geographical settings, including both national and international, in which to practice.

In addition, there is great diversity of choice in field of practice. Occupational therapists held about eighty-two thousand jobs in 2002. About one in ten occupational therapists holds more than one job. The largest number of jobs is in hospitals. Other major employers are offices of other health practitioners (including offices of occupational therapists), public and private educational services, and nursing care facilities. Some occupational therapists are employed by home health-care services, outpatient care centers, offices of physicians, individual and family services, community-care facilities for the elderly, and government agencies. Camps for handicapped children and day care for geriatric and psychiatric clients are other potential employers.

A small number of occupational therapists are self-employed in private practice. These practitioners see clients referred by physicians or other health professionals or provide contract or consulting services to nursing-care facilities, schools, adult day-care programs, and home health-care agencies.

The Clinical Therapist

The clinician is a client-centered therapist treating patients or clients whose lives have been interrupted by physical injury, disease, developmental defects, aging, mental health problems, drug abuse, or other factors.

The clinical therapist is an active practitioner who works directly with patients, either on a one-to-one basis or in a group situation. In some cases treatment takes place in the home. Home visitations are often made in conjunction with the visiting nurse or physical therapist and often working out of state social services or public health programs.

Staff Duties

The major duties of a staff occupational therapist in a hospital can be considered in three broad dimensions:

1. **Patient treatment.** This involves evaluation, goal setting, treatment, and reporting.
2. **Departmental routines.** This involves scheduling, accountability, maintenance of equipment, ordering supplies, and conducting inventories.
3. **Educational activities.** This involves supervising, orienting, advising, and presenting service and continuing education programs.

Each patient poses a different problem because no two patients are exactly alike. This diversity and variety are part of what makes occupational therapy such an exciting profession.

The American Occupational Therapy Association, Inc., gives some idea of the diversity of treatment categories in which occupational therapists and occupational therapy assistants provide service. As previously mentioned, therapists work with individuals in a number of other diagnostic categories beyond the major classifications listed below.

Most Frequent Health Problems of Patients/Clients

Physical Health Problems
Amputation
Arteriosclerosis
Arthritis/collagen disorders
Back injuries

Burns
Cancer (neoplasms)
Cardiopulmonary diseases
Cerebral palsy
Congenital anomalies
CVA/hemiplegia
Developmental delays
Diabetes
Feeding disorders
Fractures
Hand injuries
Hearing disabilities
HIV infections, including AIDS
Kidney disorders
Learning disabilities
Neuromuscular disorders (MD, MS, and so forth)
Respiratory diseases
Spinal cord injuries
Traumatic brain injuries
Visual disabilities
Well population

Mental Health Problems
Adjustment disorders
Affective disorders
Alcohol/substance use disorders
Alzheimer's disease
Anxiety disorders
Eating disorders
Mental retardation

Organic mental disorders (including dementias and organic
   brain syndromes but excluding Alzheimer's)
Personality disorders
Schizophrenic disorders
Other psychotic disorders
Other mental health disorders

Entry-Level Positions

The first entry-level job in the field is usually a staff position under
the supervision of a clinical supervisor. Progress into positions of
greater responsibility, such as student supervision and clinical teaching, becomes possible as a therapist gains job experiences and treatment competencies.

The time lapse before job promotion rests, of course, with the
therapist, depending on his or her interest, motivation, and dedi-
cation. Ascending job responsibilities occur at about two- to four-
year intervals. But job advancement may occur rapidly, based on
ability. Occupational therapy is one of the fastest-growing health
professions, making employment and advancement opportunities
excellent.

Scientific Knowledge

The occupational therapist must have a good background of scientific knowledge concerning the normal and pathological structure
and function of the human body.

Any interrupted pathways of the sensory-input or motor-output
systems will, of course, result in impaired sensorimotor responses.
The therapist is educated to be aware of symptoms indicating dys-

function. Such symptom pictures serve as the basis for preparing treatment programs incorporating purposeful activities and skill development for each patient. Learning about normal and abnormal psychological functioning and psychiatric dysfunction is also a necessary part of an occupational therapist's education. Such knowledge helps therapists understand the emotional accompaniments of both physical and psychological disorders.

Psychological Aspects of Approach

Whether the therapist is working with patients or clients in fine motor skills through activities, in job-related skills such as typing, or in neuromuscular therapy, he or she works to improve function in physical or psychological daily living skills. The patient's recovery is the primary goal. The pleasure and sense of accomplishment derived from these activities is of great psychological benefit; the end product of the activity, if any, is secondary. For example, the process of making a craft item, if used in physical dysfunction therapy, is more important by virtue of exercising and developing certain muscles than the way the finished product looks. Along with physical improvement, it is important to watch for emotional progress in patients, since both physical and psychological well-being are important components of occupational therapy. In a psychiatric facility, of course, the emotional aspect is of prime importance.

Therapist Concerns

As we have seen, whatever the condition that impedes the patient's ability to engage in and fully perform tasks of daily living, occupational therapy seeks to aid in the development of coping skills.

The primary focus of occupational therapy as a health profession is the enhancement of adaptive skills and performance capacity. Therapists are concerned with factors that are barriers to the individual's capacity to function, either mentally or physically.

The therapist must understand the patient's mental attitudes, motivating factors, and readiness for individual or group participation. Careful records are kept relative to the patient's progress from admittance to discharge. This is for the protection of both the patient or client and the therapist. In addition, careful records ensure continuity and quality of care in the event of a change in therapists or readmission.

Evaluation Techniques

To interpret evaluation findings, the clinician must have a sound knowledge of human development and the nervous system, as well as an understanding of sensorimotor integration.

Students in occupational therapy programs learn the techniques of administering various tests used for evaluation. The clinical fieldwork portion of the study program provides opportunities for gaining valuable practice in these evaluation techniques.

A few examples of areas in which occupational therapists carry out evaluations should give you a basic understanding of the types of evaluations clinicians must perform before beginning treatment. Within each of these areas there may be many specific tests from which to choose. In certain instances, therapists must devise a test to elicit the information needed to plan treatment. Although the therapist must record results in writing, the majority of tests do not involve paper and pencil responses by the patient or client. Rather, the therapist usually asks the patient to perform a task incorporating the behavior being noted or observes the individual in a naturalistic or uncontrived setting that is likely to elicit the physical, emotional, social, or cognitive-based responses pertinent to therapy. Whenever possible (depending on mental and physical condition, age, and so forth), results of the evaluation are discussed with the patient or client, and he or she is involved in setting goals for treatment. The types of evaluations occupational therapists perform are described below.

Developmental Tests

These tests are used to assess a child's gross motor, fine motor, adaptive, language, and personal-social skills. Various performance items are observed and recorded on forms that, when scored, indicate the developmental level of the child in each of the above skill areas. These tests are also sometimes helpful in assessing older developmentally delayed persons. When delays are found in one or more areas, therapy is initiated to provide developmental stimulation. Children who are hospitalized for long periods of time are likely to fall behind others in their age group unless developmentally appropriate activities are provided during hospitalization. Results of the evaluation may also be used to counsel parents on appropriate methods of enhancing development.

There are two basic types of daily living skills. Physical daily living skills evaluate the patient's ability to walk, sit, dress, accomplish self-feeding, care for personal hygiene, use the telephone, and perform other daily self-help tasks. Psychological/emotional daily living skills refer to performance in developing personal self-concept or self-identity, coping in a variety of situations, and being involved in the community or society.

Following testing, a treatment program will be planned to help the patient or client perform the activities that he or she needs and is able to perform. This may be accomplished by strengthening muscles through exercise, body positioning, performance practice, or by using adapted equipment.

Occupational therapists are well equipped to design and make adapted devices or splints for patients to aid them in the activities of daily living. Many devices are commercially available, but at times custom-made devices may be necessary.

Homemaker Evaluation

This assessment attempts to determine how well a patient can use the necessary equipment to care for a home. For example, how well is a wheelchair-bound patient able to use the stove, sink, and other kitchen equipment? Are cabinets at a level where various homemaker tools can be reached? Are there modifications that can be made to the wheelchair or to the room that would enable the patient to prepare a meal in the kitchen? Can modifications, such as handrails on the tub, be made to the bathroom? Do the patient's clothes have zippers and easy snaps that will facilitate getting dressed?

Sensorimotor Evaluation

This includes assessment of the client's ability to receive stimuli through the senses of sight, hearing, smell, taste, and touch; of his or her level of equilibrium; and of his or her ability to react to stimuli. It also implies the neurological function of interpreting the stimuli.

Study of sensory integration by many occupational therapists has resulted in the development of measurement tools, based on scientific data, with which therapists can more accurately assess cognitive, perceptual, motor, and behavioral problems. These tests are useful to the therapist in planning treatment procedures.

The last several years have seen an increase in scientific methods of measurement in the cognitive-perceptual field. While it was once not understood why a child could not interpret what he or she saw, felt, read, or heard, or why his or her sense of balance was impaired, basic scientific evaluations now are available that point the way toward a better understanding of these and other problems related to cognitive-perceptual motor processes.

Treatment is based on the selection of activities that will give practice in performing the underdeveloped function. Substitute functions also may be developed and tasks adapted by positioning of the patient and/or the use of equipment.

Range of Motion

This is a measurement of the amount of motion present at any given joint. Distance between a position of extension (straight) and a position of flexion (bent), or other motions, is measured.

If joints are stiff and show a limited range of motion, activities are selected that will exercise these joints. Conservation of diseased joints also may be a goal.

Testing Muscle Strength

This test evaluates the status of individual muscles or muscle groups—for instance, whether the muscles of the wrist are strong enough to flex and extend that joint. Progressive resistive exercises are used in treatment directed toward strengthening specific muscle groups. The goal is to improve functional ability by overcoming weakness or to help the client or patient discover alternative ways to increase independence.

Activities requiring coordination and dexterity are used to determine how well certain groups of muscles work together to produce smooth, coordinated action. Can a child get a spoon to the mouth, or is assistance needed? Coordination and dexterity measure the quickness and accuracy of a patient's ability to perform certain functional tasks.

As you have seen, the areas of function that we have considered are closely interrelated and overlap. It follows, therefore, that treatment programs are equally interrelated.

Neurodevelopmental approaches to treatment are based on developmental patterns controlled by the nervous system. Neurophysiological approaches are based on the interplay between the sensory and motor functions of the nervous system. There are many highly specialized techniques in use today to assist patients with muscle coordination and sensory problems.

Vocational Evaluation

This evaluation assesses the client's cognitive and physical abilities; work skills, habits, and interests; social adjustment; and potential employability. Partial simulation of work activities may be used. The results of these evaluations are usually made available to a vocational counselor, who may arrange for job training as indicated.

Body Image Evaluations

These evaluations determine the patient's ability for body visualization, such as locating various parts of the body relative to positioning. Following a cerebrovascular accident (stroke), the patient may have difficulty in determining his or her body position and may sustain a changed body concept because of paralysis and loss of function on one side of the body.

Personality and Object Relations

These play an important part in adjusting to daily routines of living. Therapists analyze the individual's effort and ability to carry out daily life skills in a manner that provides personal satisfaction and a productive role of satisfying living. Evaluation procedures are used to make a basic assessment of the client. Some of the personality concepts evaluated include self-concept, concept of others, communication skills, and personal conflicts. These and other areas of function are evaluated to reach a basic personality assessment of the patient or client and to aid the occupational therapist in the treatment of various emotional problems.

Object relations concerns the relationship behavior of the client with animate and inanimate things in his or her environment. This would include people, pets, plants, and inanimate objects such as toys and furniture.

The identification of problems that are preventing the patient from developing satisfactory relationships in his or her environment is the first step in helping to overcome them. Treatment may be planned as an individual activity with the therapist or as a group activity with peers, depending on the unique problems presented.

As you can see, the therapist is constantly faced with a variety of treatment situations of a physical or psychological nature. These situations can affect people at all stages of life, from the infant to the senior citizen. The occupational therapist plays an important part in health care for disabled and ill persons.

Results Documentation

The careful recording of all evaluation and treatment procedures used for any given patient or client is a requisite to quality care. Evaluation results and interpretation help occupational therapists to plan treatment and the health-care team members to make decisions regarding further treatment or outside placement. Results also aid family members in planning for care, making financial arrangements, and so forth. Not only is the therapist responsible for sharing information orally with other concerned members of the service community, but he or she also must take care in keeping the client's record. The total treatment process, therefore, encompasses the processes of evaluation, goal setting, program development, program implementation, and documentation of results.

6

WORK ENVIRONMENTS

OCCUPATIONAL THERAPISTS ARE employed in five broad categories
of agencies. These areas are: federal, state, municipal, nonprofit,
and for-profit. The services of these health-delivery centers overlap
in some instances, but generally speaking these categories cover the
broad spectrum of positions where one finds therapists at work.
Other areas of employment, such as private practice, hospice, and
Foreign Service employment, also will be discussed in this chapter.

Federal Agencies

Federal agencies employing occupational therapists include the
armed forces, with their medical specialist corps and sections. The
Department of Veterans Affairs caters to the needs of disabled veterans. The U.S. Public Health Service (USPHS) is the principal
health agency of the federal government; its main objective is to
protect and advance the health of American citizens. Because of
their expertise and knowledge of the health-care system, some occu-

pational therapists have assumed higher-level health-related positions in the federal government.

Department of Veterans Affairs Medical Centers

These centers fall under the civil service system and number more than 170 hospitals in the United States, the District of Columbia, Puerto Rico, Guam, and the Philippine Islands. They provide ongoing care with medical, surgical, rehabilitation, and psychiatric services for military veterans.

Positions are posted at the Veterans Affairs website, which you can access at www.vacareers.va.gov. Appointments for occupational therapists are made through the Office of Personnel Management. Applicants must be U.S. citizens in good health and graduates of approved programs in occupational therapy.

U.S. Army

Applicants for an occupational therapy army career must hold the minimum required degree from an approved program in occupational therapy.

The army's medical specialist corps, which includes occupational therapy, offers many opportunities to promote professional growth. As an officer and member of the army medical team, an applicant may qualify to attend several educational programs, such as the advanced officer's course or army hospital courses. Assignments in other countries are sometimes given.

In addition, the army offers the PaYS program (Partnership for Youth Success). Under PaYS, various private employers partner with the army to provide career opportunities for individuals who have gained skill and experience while serving in the army. The PaYS agreement is made at enlistment. At the completion of service, pre-selected PaYS employers will interview candidates. Hundreds of employers around the country are part of the PaYS program.

Information about army careers is available at www.goarmy.com. Visit www.armypays.com for details about PaYS.

U.S. Navy

Applicants for navy service must be fully qualified occupational therapists. This includes the minimum required entry-level degree from an accredited college or university and certification after completing an approved course in occupational therapy. Applicants must also be citizens of the United States, be physically and professionally qualified, and be at least eighteen years of age at the time of appointment.

A navy occupational therapist is part of the multidisciplinary rehabilitation team in the navy medical department. The occupational therapist plans and supervises treatment programs for patients with a wide range of physical and emotional dysfunctions. As a member of the navy medical service corps, the therapist will serve in naval hospitals throughout the United States. For more information visit www.navy.com/careers.

U.S. Air Force

The minimum educational requirements for USAF positions are a bachelor's degree and the completion of an approved course in an occupational therapy school. If accepted, assignments are made to air force medical centers and regional hospitals.

The air force uses the health-care team concept of integrating the biomedical sciences into a worldwide system. Each health-care discipline is centered in medical complexes, which are organized for clinical seminars and teaching. Each center is affiliated with a medical school program of continuing education, which is designed to keep officers abreast of current medical, psychological, and biological specializations.

Thus, the air force occupational therapist is exposed to and works with many kinds of physical and mental dysfunctions. Applicants must be at least eighteen years of age. Visit www.airforce.com for more information.

U.S. Public Health Service

As already stated, the USPHS is the principal health agency of the federal government. Its main objective is to advance the health of citizens and to conduct basic health research in designated areas of environmental medicine.

The occupational therapist will find many challenging and interesting positions in this service. Chronic diseases are studied, coordination of community services is evaluated, and new treatments for stroke, mental illness, heart disease, and other conditions are constantly tested and refined. The opportunity for the therapist in public health is a unique and meaningful one, particularly for those with an inquiring mind.

Initially the staff therapist receives a staff or outpatient assignment and thereafter progresses to a supervisory level. Certain civil service and agency requirements must, of course, be met. Some therapists work in the Peace Corps, accepting assignments in foreign countries after extensive orientation to the culture and needs of the host country. Go to www.usphs.gov to obtain more detailed information.

State Agencies

Each state has an agency for services to the physically and mentally handicapped. Under governmental jurisdictions, care has been extended to victims of cerebral palsy, birth defects, congenital heart defects, and other disabling diseases.

The objective of state services for children with special needs is to search out all children from birth on who have potentially handicapping conditions. A health team of the various disciplines, which includes occupational therapy, works to restore as much function and social organization as possible to the client. Most of the staff therapists in these programs give direct patient care, teach and counsel parents, demonstrate care and the use of braces and artificial limbs, and plan activities to restore functions. The state consultant of such a program educates staff members, evaluates their performance, and makes proper reports to the state authorities. These consultants are also active in community affairs and address various groups and explain the service programs to them.

In addition, occupational therapists are employed in state institutions designed to provide for the needs of the mentally ill and developmentally disabled.

Municipal Departments

Large general hospitals are usually found in cities and have well-equipped occupational therapy departments and staffs. Almost all medical schools are attached to general hospitals, which are usually teaching hospitals for professional students of all disciplines. All types of medical disabilities are found in this environment, together with many departments, such as orthopedic, neurological, dermatological, ophthalmological, psychiatric, and pediatric. Special clinics for patients with cerebral palsy, spina bifida, diabetes mellitus, and other conditions may exist in these hospitals.

Public schools employ many therapists to work with children having physical disabilities, learning disabilities, emotional problems, or various developmental delays.

Nonprofit and For-Profit Agencies

Nonprofit agencies are supported by private funds and endowments. Two of the largest and best-known agencies in this area are the United Cerebral Palsy Association, Inc., and the National Easter Seal Society. These agencies have a great many state affiliates that are directly involved in the delivery of health services. Nonprofit agencies offer many different types of positions in occupational therapy. Persons interested in this kind of professional work should apply directly to the affiliate organization in their respective states. For-profit agencies also employ occupational therapists in similar positions.

Rehabilitation Centers

There are many rehabilitation centers in the United States due to favorable federal legislation and the consistent and unflagging work of the national and local nonprofit agencies involved. Rehabilitation units are found in for-profit facilities as well.

Rehabilitation, as such, is not just treatment for one condition; it concerns all medical services and allied health personnel. The occupational therapist, the physical therapist, the physician, the nurse, the social worker, and other closely allied professional persons such as the psychologist, the teacher, and the vocational counselor all participate in the rehabilitation program. The patient's family members also play an important role in this process.

The philosophy of rehabilitation includes all the medical, psychosocial, and vocational aspects of the client. It means that the goals of treatment are directed toward as complete a restoration of physical function and social living as is possible for the client to achieve.

In many cases, rehabilitation procedures are under the jurisdiction of a physiatrist, who is a medical specialist in the treatment of rehabilitation medicine. However, the physiatrist is also aware of the other medical and social components present in the total rehabilitation of a client and will make referrals to other professionals as indicated.

These other professional services may come from other community facilities and medical sources. They may be in nearby hospitals, outpatient clinics, or through home visitation by public health or private home health personnel. If needed, they may also come from delivery of health services in the public school system, an area in which many occupational therapists now practice.

Some of the rehabilitation services in a community that may be within a rehabilitation center are as follows:

- Services of medical specialists
- Social services casework to assist client and family
- Physical therapy services
- Occupational therapy services for evaluation in physical, psychosocial, and vocational areas, and treatment as necessary
- Speech and hearing therapy

- Special education for the handicapped
- Psychological and counseling services
- Vocational counseling with reference to employment
- Residential clubs to adjust to outside living
- Halfway houses, which aid in the readjustment of the psychiatric client returning to the community
- Sheltered workshops and remunerative centers
- Independent living centers
- Adult day care

Industrial Clinics

Many large insurance companies maintain their own rehabilitation centers, where their clients are sent for treatment and where their progress can be watched closely. The Liberty Mutual Company of Boston has been a pioneer in this field. Multiple fractures, hand injuries, sprains, strains, dislocations, crush injuries, amputations, and ruptured discs and other back injuries are high-frequency disabilities found in many large cities. This type of industrial occupational therapy covers a broad spectrum and offers well-paid and interesting positions for the therapist. Individual therapists also have set up their own private clinics for industry-related disabilities.

Private Practice

Increasing numbers of occupational therapists are entering the rapidly expanding area of private practice. As more insurance companies provide financial coverage for occupational therapy, increasing opportunities exist for private practice therapists, whose fees are paid by third-party involvement that covers patient treatment.

Many of these therapists contract with agencies, hospitals, and physicians to provide services.

The therapist contemplating private practice should have at least three to six years of experience in a clinical specialty, a sound knowledge of business practice, and a thorough knowledge of the national, state, and local laws governing such practice. Legal and ethical procedures must be of prime concern to independent therapists in private practice, since they do not have the support and guidance of an institution in legal matters.

The therapist should have a wide acquaintance with physicians and organizations, both in medical facilities and in rehabilitation and other health-related centers. Such information should be procured in advance of soliciting clients and entering private practice. It is also advisable to meet with key local health-care personnel to ascertain whether the community can support a private practice.

Adequate insurance coverage is necessary for all parties concerned, to cover any incidents that might occur during treatment. The American Occupational Therapy Association can provide information about obtaining insurance.

Extensive equipment is necessary for private case handling. The equipment is expensive and must be paid for by the therapist running the private clinic. Maintenance expenses, such as rent, heat, light, telephone, and other incidentals, also must be calculated to give a complete expense estimate.

Hospices

Over the last several years, a positive change has occurred in society's attitude concerning the care of the dying. In the past, patients sometimes approached death without much care or understanding.

Hospices are organized for just the opposite reason: to teach the patient to learn to live with his or her terminal condition and to meet death with a degree of peace of mind. Patients in a hospice are treated as normally as possible. There are beauty salons, recreational activities, and discussion groups. Death is a subject that is discussed openly. Hospices provide understanding and kindness and encourage family interaction and participation in the patient's care and treatment.

But why mention hospices in connection with occupational therapists? Therapists receive excellent basic training in psychosocial services and are thus well equipped to deal with terminal illness and the special care required. Dying is a fact of life—one that the therapist is sure to encounter. Psychological support for terminally ill patients is an important service that occupational therapists are well qualified to provide.

Hospice care combines three concerns:

1. **Pain control.** It is a fundamental belief of the hospice that pain need not be a problem and that its adequate control should consist of the right medicinal dosage at the right time.
2. **Thoughtful personal treatment.** Hospice staff members treat the patient as a whole person. Drugs are used to relieve pain, not to prolong life. It is important in hospice care to give patients as much control over their lives as they are able to manage.
3. **Family support.** Members of the family are welcome at any time of the day or night and are urged to stay with patients if they wish.

Overseas Assignments

Some occupational therapists secure Foreign Service employment through the Peace Corps, the World Federation of Occupational Therapists, or other groups. Not everyone will want to practice abroad, but the following pointers should be helpful to those who find this idea attractive.

When accepting a foreign assignment, it is a good idea to learn as much as you can about the country in which you plan to work. Study the social customs, economic conditions, religion, history, and geography of the country and try to fit into its pattern of living. It will differ from what you are accustomed to, and you must avoid the temptation to "reform" nationals in other countries to your way of life. The well-accepted therapist working overseas is the one who tries to live as much as possible as the people in the visited areas live and does not demand preferential accommodations or other special treatment.

No matter which country you select or who is sponsoring you, you will need certain official papers: a passport, visas, a health certificate, a driver's license, and a work permit.

You will need to be immunized against diseases such as typhoid, typhus, or other diseases prevalent in the area where you will serve.

7

ADMINISTRATION

To FUNCTION EFFECTIVELY as an occupational therapist, you must understand the responsibilities and concerns of your supervisors, as well as the needs of your patients or clients. An understanding of the administrative structure of your department will be useful even to those who intend to serve in a strictly clinical capacity. This chapter will use the example of a hospital occupational therapy department to discuss administration, although many therapists are employed in wide-ranging types of administrative positions in non-hospital settings.

Duties of an Administrator

Although many therapists become administrators beyond the department level, this section will focus on the administration of occupational therapy departments. Departments of occupational therapy are organized and administered in accordance with the policies of the employing agency, which should be clearly understood by all personnel. The usual routine duties connected with the administration of a clinical department include:

- Direction and supervision of all personnel in the occupational therapy department
- Maintenance of supplies and equipment
- Maintenance of departmental records
- Responsibility for periodic reports of departmental activities
- Promotion of community relations
- Program development
- Marketing available services
- Recruiting and hiring personnel

Employment

The employment of personnel varies considerably, depending on the employment policies of the facility. In many instances, the responsibility of finding, interviewing, and hiring qualified staff lies with the department director. In other cases, all employment is done through a central personnel office, and the therapist is only asked to conduct an interview, review the records of the individual in question, and accept or reject the applicant.

Orientation

All personnel assigned to a department must be familiar with the regulations and policies of the institution and those of the department. They must clearly understand their duties and responsibilities and know what is expected of them. They must understand the organizational system of the institution and the lines of authority. For example, the staff therapist is directly responsible to the director of the department, while students or aides are responsible to the staff therapist designated to supervise students. Each occupational therapy department should have its own set of personnel policies.

Treatment Schedules

The staff therapist must also schedule the treatment of patients, and the supervisor must see that the patient load is equitably divided among staff members. The therapist must know when a patient will be available for treatment, schedule the patient, and check to be sure that the patient reports at the scheduled time.

Conferences

All departments, whether large or small, should arrange periodic conferences for all personnel. This is the director's responsibility. Some departments have conferences for fifteen minutes or so every morning, others once a week at a regularly scheduled time, and others meet only once a month. Usually these conferences include departmental policy changes, problems of expansion and supply, and specific patient problems. In this way, all personnel are promptly notified of any new developments, and all have responsibility for contributing to the planning of the group.

A departmental director or supervisor should also arrange to have individual supervisory conferences periodically with each member of the staff. These conferences are used to evaluate work performance, to discuss program development in each therapist's specialty area, and to hear concerns of personnel. The director should always be available to give help and guidance as needed.

Morale

Maintaining good morale and having solid working relationships with your staff are important. The wise therapist will be supportive of all staff members, affording equal privileges and opportunities for everyone and showing no favoritism. A policy of this kind will help avoid petty jealousies and grudges among staff members.

Supplies and Equipment Maintenance

The administrative duties of the therapist relative to the maintenance of supplies and equipment include ordering or purchasing, maintaining inventories, and seeing to the care and repair of equipment. Equipment refers to nonexpendable items that require replacement only after hard use or loss.

Sliding Inventory

To know what supplies are on hand and when it is necessary to reorder, a carefully maintained stock-sliding inventory must be kept. Likewise, an inventory of nonexpendable equipment is necessary, because the therapist is responsible to the institution for all equipment consigned for the department's use and must report all lost or worn-out items.

Monthly Reports

The therapist usually needs to submit a monthly report or summary of all activities within the department. Departmental records form the basis for such a report: patient treatment statistics; personnel changes; new procedures that have been instituted during the period; any changes that have taken place; special events that have been planned for patients (picnics, outings, parties, holiday events); visitors to the department; newly acquired equipment; and educational activities and seminars. Productivity reporting and quality assurance activities help ensure effective treatment at reasonable cost. This information is usually incorporated into an annual report that is submitted to the director, who in turn submits a master annual report. In both academic and clinical situations, the director of occupational therapy submits an annual budget to the institution's management.

Medical Charts

The therapist has access to the patient's medical chart. This is privileged information and should not be discussed with the patient or others. If the patient or family desire information about the medical record, they should ask the physician directly.

Ward Rounds

The therapist may spend a part of each day accompanying physicians on ward rounds or in clinical visitations. At this time, new patients are examined and treatments are prescribed. Progress is noted in patients undergoing treatment. Physicians also may advise necessary changes in treatment procedures.

Staff Conferences

Staff conferences of various kinds are usually held in institutions and agencies, and perhaps the most helpful ones to the therapist are those that have to do with patients. All members of the staff meet to discuss the problems of specific patients, with each member reporting on the progress made. These conferences highlight the collaborative efforts of many specialists who are working to bring the greatest benefit to the patient. Problems are discussed, treatment emphases are changed, or the group may decide that maximum benefit has been achieved.

Multidisciplinary Approach to Treatment

Another consideration in the planning of a treatment program is the correlation of occupational therapy with other therapies being administered. Staff conferences, which were discussed above, are an important means of correlation.

The therapist should know not only which other departments are treating the patient, but also what goals they are working toward, when treatments are scheduled, and the length of each daily treatment. For example, if a patient is receiving treatment in physical therapy for restoration of function in a stiff elbow joint, the occupational therapist should know what exercises are prescribed and how they are being done. The same motion can then be carried over into the occupational therapy treatment.

Evaluation of Treatment

The therapist must watch for signs of fatigue or for any contraindications to treatment. The therapist also observes signs of change in the physical or mental attitudes, for these may indicate a need for changes in treatment.

Treatment must be evaluated according to changes in the patient's condition. This may mean longer or shorter work periods, increasing or decreasing the physical demands of the work and the amount of coordination required, and increasing concentration, mental effort, and responsibility. If there appear to be indications for a change of total treatment goals, then the therapist must confer with the physician and other team members and proceed in accordance with revised goals. Therapists may conduct research to investigate the results of individual or group patient treatment; these data provide valuable information relative to quality of patient care.

Community Relations

The importance of establishing and maintaining a good working relationship with all patients and personnel of the agency makes community relations an important part of an occupational therapist's work. A satisfactory and congenial relationship requires thought and continuing action. It is accomplished by friendliness, courtesy, respect, and consideration for others and for their rights.

Good community relations must be maintained not only with the institutional "family," so to speak, but also with all visitors to the institution with whom the therapist comes into contact. The administrative therapist acts as host to any visitors to the clinic and must explain to them as clearly as possible the functions of the profession. Building and maintaining good public relations is a duty not only within the walls of the institution, but also in all contacts with the community at large. The therapist must always represent not only herself or himself but also serve the profession and the employing facility. The goodwill created reflects upon all three.

Community Services

The community in which the department is located becomes a potential source of diversified help to the therapist and patients; therefore, it is important to acquire as much knowledge of these resources as possible. Among the first things that a therapist should learn about are the various services within the community that can be used for the benefit of the patient. What other resources, such as sheltered workshops, homebound services, rehabilitation centers, vocational rehabilitation centers, employment services, senior citizen groups, and youth training opportunities, for example, are available to the patient?

If clients need vocational rehabilitation, the therapist should have knowledge of the job opportunities within the community. What are the local industries? What jobs in these industries might be open to patients? How many people are already trained to do these jobs? For example, it would be foolish to encourage a patient toward an interest in computer repair if there are already too many such workers for the community to support.

Aside from the many sources that may be tapped for the direct benefit of the patient, there are others that may broaden the scope of the occupational therapy program and provide indirect help to the occupational therapist. For example, the community itself is the source for volunteer help. If the therapist wants volunteer help in the department, it is necessary to determine whether community residents are interested in volunteering. The therapist should also know if the organizational machinery is already in place for the recruitment and training of volunteers or if establishment of a program is necessary.

The public library is another valuable source of aid, as is the art museum, if one is nearby. Both have resource materials that may be borrowed and staff who are in a position to advise and help the therapist.

Professional Promotion

Each graduate therapist is charged with the responsibility of utilizing every possible opportunity to clearly and correctly interpret the functions of the profession. We have seen that occupational therapy is a growing and changing profession that must be constantly interpreted to members of the medical profession and to the lay public alike. Interpretation may be done verbally during casual conversations and by lectures, demonstrations, written articles, or films.

Within the institution where the therapist is employed, he or she should accept invitations to discuss the profession of occupational therapy with various groups. New staff physicians should be invited to visit the occupational therapy department during treatment periods so that the proper use of the department may be explained and demonstrated. New interns and residents and house doctors should be contacted and introduced to the department as soon as possible after their arrival. The therapist will have frequent opportunity to give orientation lectures to nurses, attendants, and other personnel.

The therapist will be invited to lecture to various community groups regarding the purposes of the profession and the educational requirements to enter it. As mentioned previously, many of these groups will visit the institution and tour the department.

Educational Duties

The actual educational duties of the administrative therapist will depend on whether he or she is employed in a teaching hospital or whether, for training purposes, the department of occupational therapy is affiliated with an accredited educational program in occupational therapy. (See Chapter 8 for additional information on teaching positions.)

Clinical Affiliations/Fieldwork

If the department is a clinical education center for occupational therapy students, the clinical teaching program will be arranged for varying lengths of time for each disability area designated, depending on what arrangements are made with the school. In any event, the students are there for a specific period of time. Early in their educational program, students may merely observe or perform simple duties in line with their current level of skills. The final level of fieldwork, sometimes called an *internship* or *affiliation*, requires the baccalaureate student to spend six months, full-time, in one or more professional settings. During this time the student gains a minimum of three months of supervised experience in physical dysfunction and three months in psychosocial dysfunction. The responsibilities of the supervising therapist include planning the student's work schedule; arranging for attendance at clinics, staff meetings, and any special lectures or demonstrations; organizing field trips to nearby institutions and community agencies; teaching treatment procedures; and supervising and guiding the student as treatment is given.

Volunteers

Volunteers are another group that may add to the educational responsibilities of the therapist. If the institution approves the use of volunteers in the occupational therapy department, and no training facilities exist in the community, the therapist will have to organize a training course. Volunteers must receive instruction regarding the policies of the agency and department. They must know general precautions to be observed if they are to have direct patient contact. Finally, the therapist must teach them the skills and activities in which their aid is needed. The therapist has full responsibility for volunteers as they work in the clinical settings, with responsibility for their errors as well as for their services.

8

ADDITIONAL PROFESSIONAL OPPORTUNITIES

THERE ARE SEVERAL opportunities in occupational therapy aside from those in the clinical and administrative areas. In this chapter we will examine careers in teaching, research, consulting, community health care, and public schools.

Teaching

A purveyor of knowledge, an attentive listener, and a sympathetic counselor—these are the attributes of a good teacher. Teaching in an academic program that prepares occupational therapists is not an easy job. The demands are constant, and you must be a dedicated person with a genuine desire to teach and the enthusiasm to impart knowledge to students. The ability to stimulate students to think independently, to be problem solvers, and to make good value judgments is a rare quality.

Teaching is an art, but scientific findings can be of practical value in helping the teacher to better understand students and to modify personal attitudes and behaviors based on more astute observations. Research findings may provide insight into better ways of presenting material.

Effective teaching takes a great deal of preparation. For each hour of teaching, two or three hours must be spent in routine preparation procedures. This involves preparing course objectives and schedules; writing and giving examinations; grading papers; and, one of the most rewarding aspects of teaching, student conferences, where one gains insight to students' thinking. Occupational therapy faculty members in most institutions of higher learning are expected to conduct research and to publish in their areas of expertise. These are common requirements for promotion and tenure in colleges and universities.

Teaching occupational therapy provides a unique professional opportunity for the person who really wants to teach, either academically or clinically. You must enjoy teaching, and if you teach well, your students will catch your enthusiasm at once. An effective teacher guides students to active involvement in the learning process. You are influencing young minds, molding them into a firmer shape. This is one of the greatest satisfactions of teaching.

Teaching appointments in colleges or universities are usually of an academic nature with the rank of instructor, assistant professor, associate professor, or full professor. Clinical supervisors of field experience may hold academic appointments as adjunct instructors if affiliated with a school program. Teaching ranks and titles vary with the different academic organization of colleges and universities. The descriptions in this chapter are limited primarily to entry-level academic and clinical teaching, but teaching experienced therapists in postprofessional master's degree programs also is possible for those with the necessary experience and advanced education.

Academic teaching in a school usually includes the basic and social sciences applied to occupational therapy, plus instruction in therapeutic activities, while clinical teaching involves translating theory into practice by treating patients under the supervision of a registered therapist. Student field practice is arranged by the school faculty and includes a total of six to nine months of experience in the various clinical areas of occupational therapy under the auspices of approved affiliation centers.

A student performance evaluation report is kept on all occupational therapy students working in the field. This report is later discussed with the student by both the clinical supervisor and the supervisor of affiliation in the academic program.

Two important positions in occupational therapy education that fall outside the realm of "pure" teaching are the program director and the fieldwork coordinator. Both play significant roles in educating today's therapists.

Occupational Therapy Program Director

The occupational therapy program director represents the facility to the administrators of the educational institution. The program may be at a university, college, or technical school, as in the case of some occupational therapy assistant programs. The director must possess wide knowledge of occupational therapy theory and practice. He or she must be a registered occupational therapist and have attained at least a master's degree, and more appropriately a doctoral degree.

School administrators have many roles, but foremost among them is that of program developer. The tangible responsibilities are many and varied. Administrators may be asked to submit a floor plan for a new unit or select new equipment for the facility on short notice. They must work with the appropriate administrators in establishing a budget and then work within that budget. They must be familiar with business procedures such as setting up equitable pay scales and job descriptions and compiling forms for referrals and records for billing and inventory.

In addition to the proper academic credentials, the occupational therapy program director also must have the personal attributes needed for coping with the myriad problems inherent in the position. He or she must have an even temperament and the ability to make decisions and must maintain an impartial relationship with faculty and students. Working under extreme pressure is sometimes required and must be accomplished with a dignified and controlled image. In short, the director must be a leader.

The director is responsible for all departmental planning, the delegation of authority, and seeing that the work gets done. She or he attends upper-level departmental meetings, relays information back to the faculty, and conducts staff meetings to discuss school problems relative to teaching programs, the curriculum, disciplinary actions, and other pertinent affairs associated with student education.

The educational program director must enforce all school and institutional rules. Conversely, there is an obligation to staff members to communicate their problems to the administration and to back them up in their requests to be heard. An open-door policy of free communication with staff and students must be maintained.

The director plans and assigns all of the teaching assignments and negotiates faculty contracts. The director is also responsible for student placements in clinical affiliations during the students' field practice, although the actual task may be delegated to another faculty member.

Fieldwork Coordinator

The fieldwork coordinator of an educational program selects facilities for clinical education and assigns students to them for fieldwork experiences. He or she serves as the liaison between the educational program and the institution, providing the clinical experience, monitoring progress, solving problems, and so forth. Institutions with larger staffs customarily have a clinician designated as the student supervisor. Evaluation forms are prepared for each student, and these forms reflect the student's performance in the clinical situation. The completed forms are sent to the fieldwork coordinators at individual students' schools.

Clinical Research

Active research is part of the everyday professional life of the occupational therapist. It is this acquisition of knowledge through research, and the subsequent dissemination of knowledge through publication, that establishes the basic literature so necessary for the profession to grow in stature.

Research is not a "do-it-yourself" activity. One must train for the exacting science of systematic investigation, learning how to conduct research and joining forces with established investigators to compare results and procedures. Some techniques the prospective researcher must acquire are how to construct a problem statement, how to form a hypothesis, how to set up a research design to prove or disprove the hypothesis, how to analyze data, how to use basic statistics, and how to present the results in a formal written report.

For those qualified and interested, occupational therapy offers an endless source of material for investigation. Researchers in occupational therapy are now concerning themselves with some of the following questions:

- How do the results of developmental testing correlate with perceptual performance?
- How do elderly patients or clients with dementia function on selected sensory integrative measures?
- How would depressed psychotics react to organized leisure-type activities as compared to work activities?
- How do sensorimotor integrative problems affect certain aspects of life functioning, including school performance?
- What are the most effective therapy techniques for patients with specific neuromuscular problems?

Whether you participate actively in research efforts or simply keep up with new developments through reading the journals, clinical research will be an important part of your professional career.

Consultant

A consultant is a person with considerable expertise on a particular subject or situation who is called in to offer suggestions on how to improve a situation or to comment on changes already made. The consultant does not provide continuing direct care but rather provides advice to the therapist or the facility requesting assistance.

It should be kept in mind that consultants do not have mandated authority. They do not order things to be changed. They advise, comment, and suggest. Usually the employing facility receives a written report upon completion of the consultancy, and the suggestions may or may not be implemented.

Basic to successful consultation is the easy-mannered and self-controlled approach. Consultants listen a lot, do some investigating, and balance out the situation before offering advice. A great deal of tact and discretion is required in commenting and offering advice. The role of the consultant is characterized by the individual's specialized knowledge. The consultant is an outsider who tries to offer a clearer view of a situation.

Extended-care facilities and nursing homes regularly employ consultants in many areas. Most consultants have a minimum of five years of administrative clinical experience in a variety of situations, including some teaching and supervision.

Often a consultant is asked to assist in organizing a new department. This might include a number of tasks ranging from suggesting floor space and office allocations to devising record-keeping systems. In developing an initial program of treatment, consultants are frequently asked to coach the clinical staff in various procedures for handling patients.

Another type of consultant is the therapist with a basic knowledge of developmental learning materials. This type of consultancy usually takes place in educational workshops and seminars. Other consultants have expertise in sensorimotor treatment techniques, wheelchair positioning and adaptation, psychiatric treatment programming, work hardening programs, and additional areas too numerous to mention.

Community Health Care

There is an increased public awareness of the benefits of total rehabilitation in connection with such disabling conditions as birth defects, arthritis, geriatric problems, amputations, and other chronic conditions requiring long-term care. Close cooperation is required between the professional, public, and private agencies concerned with this total rehabilitation process.

The active involvement of occupational therapy professionals in community projects has been a growing trend in the last decade, and it continues to grow in importance in the field of social medicine and psychological services, as well as in preventive medicine.

Therapists are increasingly holding positions at the state level as consultants in home health-care programs. They participate in these programs as team members whose major concern is the maintenance of health and the prevention of disease and disability. Families have to be educated in the dos and don'ts of home care by means of public educational programs. In many instances, the health of patients has been restored to the point where adequate maintenance of their conditions can be sustained in the home setting, if adequate professional supervision is available.

The team members of a nursing staff and home-care aides provide continuing health-care services in the home. Their goal is to prevent further hospitalization or the recurrence of disease or disability. Occupational therapists, physical therapists, nurses, speech pathologists, nutritionists, and other specialists all contribute to such a program. Nutritional requirements are a very important issue in a home-care program to ensure that the patient receives well-balanced meals specific to his or her condition.

Other community centers include drug and alcohol abuse facilities that are established specifically for these conditions and are sometimes housed in a rehabilitation center. Much preventive work is being done in these areas.

Interim and halfway houses for the recovering client who has had a mental illness are now quite numerous and provide a sheltering atmosphere of understanding and guidance for the client until he or she is ready to face, once again, the full reality of social living. When recovering from the emotional and social problems that mental illness presents, these persons need supportive therapy for quite some time to gain a sense of security before striking out on their own.

There are also many large regional medical centers for long-term clients such as stroke, cancer, and cardiac patients who need weekly checkups and follow-up care. Occupational therapists are members of the health-care teams that serve these clients at home and on an outpatient basis.

Public Schools

Laws mandating education and special services for all handicapped children have increased the need and demand for occupational therapy in public school systems. Schools are at present the second-largest employers of occupational therapists, after hospitals.

Occupational therapists have become specialists in areas dealing with limitations in skills and abilities related to learning. In addition to the customary physical and psychosocial assessments, they regularly evaluate for problems in areas such as visual tracking, convergence abilities, discrimination of figure-ground patterns, and reverse reading problems.

Occupational therapists in schools focus on abilities needed for learning activities. Movement and coordination needed for handwriting, perceptual skills important for reading, tolerance for sitting, and other abilities are all important. Occupational therapists counsel teachers and parents, recommending special equipment or activities that will help each child function at his or her best. In school settings, therapists participate in school meetings, help develop individual educational plans, and generally become a part of the educational system. Their hours and pay are generally comparable to those of teachers in the same setting.

Occupational therapists also can give teachers in-service training seminars within the school setting to help them learn how to position children with special needs, assist them in self-feeding, and adapt school equipment. Therapists also may be able to provide insight into neurologically based learning and attention and behavior disorders. Local school systems have in recent years added many ancillary services of this type to their programs. Counselors, psychologists, speech pathologists, physical therapists, and occupational therapists have become integral parts of many public school programs.

The occupational therapist working in a community health program can become directly involved with other members of the health team, such as the public health nurse, in the detection of school-related problems. Occupational therapists in the schools are partners with other related services personnel, teachers, and administrators in the important task of providing the most appropriate environment and services for each child.

Miscellaneous Areas

As health insurance companies investigate necessary service coverage, they sometimes find a need for full-time therapists to provide advice. The same is true of employment agencies that place therapists. Some therapists start employment agencies for health professionals. Others, seeing the need for continuing education for health professionals, work full-time in setting up seminars and workshops.

Occupational therapists have developed businesses that establish contracts with hospitals and nursing homes to provide therapy services; they have become owners or employees of health product and therapy equipment companies; and they have become medical illustrators, writers, and editors. Indeed, their individual backgrounds and experience suit them for an astonishing variety of opportunities.

9

PROFESSIONAL SOCIETIES, EARNINGS, AND BENEFITS

THERE ARE PROFESSIONAL associations that are also the standard-bearers for the field of occupational therapy. In this chapter we will consider the roles of these societies and the benefits of membership. We will also consider salaries and fringe benefits for both registered occupational therapists and certified occupational therapy assistants.

The American Occupational Therapy Association, Inc.

Established in 1917, the American Occupational Therapy Association (AOTA) is the national professional organization for those who teach and practice occupational therapy. The association promotes better understanding of the profession and safeguards its standards of education and practice. It sponsors research and maintains communication with the membership and allied professions. In 2005, total membership was more than thirty-five thousand, including occupational therapists, occupational therapy assistants, and occupational therapy students. Members reside in all fifty states, the District of Columbia, Puerto Rico, and in fifty-eight foreign countries.

The national headquarters in Bethesda, Maryland, is a liaison between state and regional associations. It provides a variety of regular and special services to members and maintains educational services for the benefit of students, teachers, colleges, universities, and student affiliation centers.

The American Occupational Therapy Certification Board (AOTCB) administers the national certification examination for professional-level qualification for occupational therapist (OTR) and the proficiency examination for the assistant-level qualification (COTA). It also maintains the registry of the American Occupational Therapy Association, which includes the names of all registered occupational therapists in the United States and a list of all certified occupational therapy assistants.

The certification process for either an OTR or a COTA assures the public, physicians, hospitals, patients, and fellow therapists of the individual's professional qualification to practice. It is the final step in the process of indicating competence for entry-level practice. The association sets standards for occupational therapy practice and assists new members in developing skills for monitoring quality of care.

An annual American Occupational Therapy Association conference is held in various geographical regions of the United States. The conference brings together thousands of therapists to learn from presentations and exhibits and to share ideas. (See Appendix B for the address and phone number of the AOTA and other related professional associations.)

AOTA Goals

The goals of the American Occupational Therapy Association include the following:

1. To provide opportunities for the expression of members' concerns, to anticipate emerging issues to facilitate decision making, and to expedite the translation of these decisions into actions
2. To support the development of research and knowledge bases for the practice of occupational therapists and to promote the dissemination of such information
3. To facilitate and support an educational system for occupational therapy that responds to current health needs and anticipates, plans for, and accommodates change
4. To promote occupational therapy as a viable health profession
5. To facilitate the formation of partnerships with consumers to promote optimum health conditions for the public

Affiliations

There are approximately fifty-two AOTA regional and state affiliates. These are the local professional and regional organizations, and they carry the names of the states that they cover in their organizational charters. Each affiliate is represented in the representative assembly, which meets once a year at the national conference.

Membership Services

The American Occupational Therapy Association provides the following membership services:

- Subscription to the *American Journal of Occupational Therapy*, the peer-reviewed journal of professional research, and AJOT Online
- *OT Practice*, a biweekly news and employment publication
- *1-Minute Update*, a biweekly online news service
- Evidence Briefs and Evidence-Based Directory, which are Web-based resources and tutorials that allow users to search and interpret literature
- Eleven special-interest section newsletters
- *Journal of Occupational Therapy Students*
- Annual AOTA conference
- Loan materials relative to career education, films, and visual aids
- Assistance in the implementation of administrative and clinical practice
- Assistance in recruitment and publicity
- Assistance in establishing educational and clinical administration policies
- Resource and consultation service regarding practice and related matters
- List of publications available to members at discount rates
- Staff support in legal and legislative issues of importance to occupational therapy professionals
- Sponsorship of continuing educational institutes and workshops
- Assistance to educational programs of occupational therapy through special studies in curriculum and teaching methods
- Occupational therapy library in the AOTA national office, which includes computerized search services for a small fee
- Access to an online computerized information system

- Employment benefit program, including computerized job bank, employment exchange, placement information, direct-mail service, weekly employment bulletin
- Recognition program to grant awards for outstanding professional contributions
- Development of technical professional manuals for the use of students and other personnel
- Financial benefits program offering scholarships, fellowships, student loans, and grants
- Visitations for accrediting occupational therapy programs
- Insurance benefits program

Special-Interest Sections

Members of the American Occupational Therapy Association may choose to belong to one or more special-interest sections, each of which pertains to one area of occupational therapy practice. These include the following sections:

- Administration and management (including private practice)
- Developmental disabilities
- Education
- Gerontology
- Home and community health
- Mental health
- Physical disabilities
- School system
- Sensory integration
- Technology
- Work programs

These groups, through their leadership and the contributions of members, promote knowledge and skill development in specialized areas of practice. This role is fulfilled through informative publications, research, and the promotion of continuing education. Special-interest section members also act as liaisons to several of the national committees and advise the national office staff and the president of the national association on practice-related issues and publications.

World Federation of Occupational Therapists

The World Federation of Occupational Therapists (WFOT) is the key international representative organization for occupational therapists and is the official organization for the promotion of occupational therapy. Founded in 1952, the WFOT currently has sixty member associations around the globe. Occupational therapists with an interest in overseas employment may obtain information from the WFOT.

The objectives of the federation are:

1. To act as the official international organization for the promotion of occupational therapy; to hold international congresses
2. To promote international cooperation among occupational therapy associations, among occupational therapists, and between them and other allied professional groups
3. To maintain the ethics of the profession and to advance the practice and standards of occupational therapy
4. To promote internationally recognized standards for the education of occupational therapists

5. To facilitate the international exchange and placement of therapists and students
6. To facilitate the exchange of information and publications and to promote research

The WFOT is liaison with the World Health Organization and other nongovernmental international health organizations such as UNICEF, UNESCO, and the World Confederation of Physical Therapists.

Membership

Qualified occupational therapists and occupational therapy students can become members of the WFOT through their national organization. The WFOT website provides links to each member country, with a list of recognized educational programs in each country. Members receive the WFOT *Bulletin*. Visit www.wfot.org for complete information on member countries.

The WFOT website offers job listings, information about educational programs, and access to a variety of publications relevant to the profession.

Earnings in the Occupational Therapy Field

Most occupational therapists work for an annual salary, although some work on an hourly or *per diem* (so much per day) basis. Therapists in private practice are in a special class; their earnings are more difficult to estimate. There are substantial variations in salary among occupational therapy personnel who perform similar functions. This seems to be due, in part, to the different pay scales existing in the various geographic regions of the United States. The cost of living also varies from place to place, so you should consider a job offer in the context of the cost of living in that area. In general, occupational therapists are on a salary level comparable to other health-care professionals with similar training.

According to the U.S. Bureau of Labor Statistics, median annual earnings of occupational therapists were $54,660 in 2004. The middle 50 percent earned between $45,690 and $67,010. The lowest 10 percent earned less than $37,430, and the highest 10 percent earned more than $81,600. Median annual earnings in the industries employing the largest numbers of occupational therapists in 2004 were as follows:

Home health-care services	$58,720
Offices of other health practitioners	$56,620
Nursing-care facilities	$56,570
General medical and surgical hospitals	$55,710
Elementary and secondary schools	$48,580

According to the Bureau of Labor Statistics, the median annual earnings of occupational therapy assistants were $38,430 in 2004. The middle 50 percent earned between $31,790 and $44,390 a year. The lowest 10 percent earned less than $25,880, and the highest 10 percent earned more than $52,700 a year. Median annual earnings of occupational therapy assistants were $40,130 in offices of other health practitioners, which includes offices of occupational therapists.

Median annual earnings of occupational therapist aides were $23,150 in 2004. The middle 50 percent earned between $19,080 and $31,910. The lowest 10 percent earned less than $15,820, and the highest 10 percent earned more than $41,560.

Fringe Benefits

Benefits can be a deciding factor when faced with choosing one position over another with a similar salary. It is quite possible that five job offers with exactly the same salary would offer five different benefit packages, so it is important that you become familiar with the following typical benefits and learn how to weigh them one against another.

- **Salary review.** After accepting a position at a certain starting salary, when would you come up for a salary review? In six months? A year? Longer? Is there a set schedule of salary increments?
- **Vacation.** Are your vacations paid? How much vacation will you be eligible for after one year of service? After five years? Can some portion of your salaried vacation be taken before the end of the term, based on accrued time? Can vacation time be saved up over two or more years, or must it be taken when due?
- **Sick leave.** How many days of sick leave may you take in one year? Are they paid? What happens if you exceed this limit?
- **Authorized absences.** Are you allotted a certain number of personal days per year? How many? What about leaves of absence for pregnancy or professional development? Do you receive any portion of your salary during these absences?
- **Advancement.** Are there clearly defined criteria for professional advancement? What additional titles, duties, and responsibilities would be open to you after several years of service? Is there room to move up into more responsible positions within the organization? Given the proper

credentials, could you move freely from the clinical realm into administration or education?

- **Continuing education.** Are there any provisions for partial or total reimbursement for additional course work through graduate courses or continuing education seminars? Are your expenses for attending meetings and conferences paid? Are annual dues and membership fees for professional associations paid?
- **Malpractice.** Are you covered by insurance in case of malpractice suits?
- **Retirement.** Is there a pension plan or some other retirement program that you can participate in? What must you contribute? What are the benefits?
- **Health insurance.** Are there programs available to pay for your own personal health care? How much must you contribute?

In addition to salary and fringe benefits, other considerations such as work schedule, geographic location, and compatibility with personal circumstances also will play a part in your job evaluation.

10

OCCUPATIONAL THERAPY IN CANADA

OCCUPATIONAL THERAPY IN Canada is a closely regulated profession that strives to employ the most highly qualified individuals. Every province has a regulatory organization that is responsible for overseeing the practice of the profession. Each provincial organization sets its own regulatory requirements, and some of them require successful completion of a certification exam (see below for certification information).

The website for the Canadian Association of Occupational Therapists (CAOT) provides a link to the provincial associations. Contact information for CAOT is listed at the end of the chapter.

Educational Requirements

The board of directors of the Canadian Association of Occupational Therapists has announced that effective 2010, a professional master's degree will be the minimum entry requirement to the field.

As of 2008, CAOT will grant accreditation only to those occupational therapy programs that lead to a professional master's degree.

As of this writing, all occupational therapy programs offered by Canadian universities have instituted a professional entry-level master's program or are moving toward that goal. Following is a list of universities in Canada and the degrees that are currently awarded. The dates in parentheses represent when the university is expected to complete its move to the entry-level master's program. Check with each school to find out the status of its program changes.

Dalhousie University
School of Occupational Therapy
5869 University Avenue
Forrest Building, Room 215
Halifax, NS B3H 3J5
www.occtherapy.dal.ca
M.Sc.

McGill University
School of Physical and Occupational Therapy
3654 Prom Sir William Osler
Montreal, QC H3G 1Y5
www.medicine.mcgill.ca/spot
B.Sc. (2006)

McMaster University
School of Rehabilitation Science
Institute for Applied Health Sciences, Room 402
1400 Main Street West
Hamilton, ON L8S 1C7
www.fhs.mcmaster.ca/rehab
M.Sc.

Queen's University
School of Rehabilitation Therapy
Louise D. Acton Building
31 George Street
Kingston, ON K7L 3N6
www.rehab.queensu.ca
M.Sc.

Université Laval
Québec G1K 7P4
www.ulaval.ca
B.Sc. (2008)

University of Alberta
Department of Occupational Therapy
Faculty of Rehabilitation Medicine
2-64 Corbett Hall
Edmonton, AB T6G 2G4
www.rehabmed.ualberta.ca/ot
B.Sc., M.Sc. (2008)

University of British Columbia
School of Rehabilitation Sciences
Division of Occupational Therapy
T325-2211 Wesbrook Mall
Vancouver, BC V6T 2B5
www.rehab.ubc.ca
M.Sc.

University of Manitoba
School of Medical Rehabilitation
R106-772 McDermot Avenue
Winnipeg, MB R3E 0T6
www.umanitoba.ca/medrehab
M.Sc.

University of Montreal
School of Rehabilitation
2375 Chemin de la Côte Sainte-Catherine
Montréal, QB H3T 1A8
www.umontreal.ca
M.Sc., Ph.D.

University of Montreal
School of Rehabilitation
P.O. Box 6128, Station Centre-Ville
Montreal, QC H3C 3J7
www.umontreal.ca
B.Sc. (2007)

University of Ottawa
School of Rehabilitation Sciences
Tabaret Hall
75 Laurier Avenue East
Ottawa, ON K1N 6N5
www.health.uottawa.ca
B.Sc.

University of Toronto
Department of Occupational Science and Occupational Therapy
160-500 University Avenue
Toronto, ON M5G 1V7
www.ot.utoronto.ca
M.Sc.

University of Western Ontario
School of Occupational Therapy
Faculty of Health Sciences
Elborn College, Room 2555
London, ON N6G 1H1
www.uwo.ca
M.Sc.

Canadian Association of Occupational Therapists

The Canadian Association of Occupational Therapists is the national body that regulates the profession. Established in 1926, CAOT now has a membership of more than seventy-two hundred. CAOT works closely with the provincial professional associations and the Canadian Occupational Therapy Foundation, as well as with educational/training programs and other occupational therapy organizations.

CAOT administers a certification exam for occupational therapists. The exam is offered twice a year, in July and November, at locations throughout the country. Successful completion of the certification exam is required by some of the provincial regulatory organizations. Those who wish to take the exam must be graduates either from accredited occupational therapy programs in Canada or from programs recognized by the World Federation of Occupational Therapists.

Passing the certification examination is one of three requirements for individual membership in CAOT. The other criteria are graduation from an accredited program as mentioned above, and Canadian citizenship or official authorization to practice occupational therapy in Canada with payment of appropriate CAOT membership fees.

CAOT Membership Levels

Membership in CAOT is available at several levels. These are:

- Full-time member
- Part-time member working fewer than eight hundred hours a year
- Full-time graduate student member
- Retired member, nonpracticing
- Practicing member outside of Canada

Benefits of CAOT Membership

Membership in the Canadian Association of Occupational Therapists carries certain benefits. Included among those benefits are:

- Use of the OT(C) designation, which indicates fulfillment of CAOT membership standards and enhances professional credibility
- Eligibility for grants and scholarships from the Canadian Occupational Therapy Foundation

- Recognition of outstanding service and practice through CAOT awards
- Discounts on all conferences, courses, and publications
- Subscription to *Canadian Journal of Occupational Therapy* and *Occupational Therapy Now*
- Insurance coverage and legal advice
- Access to members-only Web resources

Contact CAOT for more detailed information on the topics discussed in this chapter:

Canadian Association of Occupational Therapists
CTTC Building, Suite 3400
1125 Colonel By Drive
Ottawa, ON K1S 5R1
caot.ca

Appendix A

Educational Programs

The following occupational therapy and occupational therapy assistant programs are accredited by the Accreditation Council for Occupational Therapy Education of the American Occupational Therapy Association, Inc. Contact the schools directly for specific information.

Occupational Therapy Programs

Key

M	professional entry-level master's degree
B/M	combined baccalaureate/master's degree
P	entry-level Ph.D. degree
C	certificate
D	is developing programs that are accepting students and has applied for accreditation

Alabama

Alabama State University (M, D)
Occupational Therapy Program
915 S. Jackson St.
Montgomery, AL 36101-0271
www.alasu.edu

Tuskegee University (M)
Occupational Therapy Program
Basil O'Connor Hall
Tuskegee, AL 36088-1696
www.tuskegee.edu

University of Alabama (M)
Department of Occupational Therapy
School of Health Related Professions
1530 3rd Ave. South, RMSB 354
Birmingham, AL 35294-1212
www.uab.edu/occupationaltherapy

University of South Alabama (M, B/M)
Department of Occupational Therapy
Springhill Academic Campus
1504 Springhill Ave., Rm. 5108
Mobile, AL 36604-3273
www.usouthal.edu

Arizona

Arizona School of Health Sciences (M)
Occupational Therapy Program
5850 E. Still Circle
Mesa, AZ 85206-3618
www.ashs.edu

Midwestern University (M)
Occupational Therapy Program
19555 N. 59th Ave.
Glendale, AZ 85308-6814
www.midwestern.edu

Arkansas

University of Central Arkansas (M, B/M)
Department of Occupational Therapy
201 Donaghey Ave., HSC Ste. 300
Box 5001
Conway, AR 72035-0001
www.uca.edu/divisions/academics/chas/ot.htm

California

California State University–Dominguez Hills (M)
Occupational Therapy Program
College of Health and Human Services
1000 E. Victoria St., WHA 320 H
Carson, CA 90747-0005
www.csudh.edu

Dominican University of California (M, B/M)
Department of Occupational Therapy
50 Acacia Ave.
San Rafael, CA 94901-2298
www.dominican.edu

Loma Linda University (M, B/M)
Occupational Therapy Program
Nichol Hall, Rm. A901
Loma Linda, CA 92350-0001
www.llu.edu

Samuel Merritt College (M)
Occupational Therapy Department
370 Hawthorne Ave.
Oakland, CA 94609-3108
www.samuelmerritt.edu

San Jose State University (M, B/M)
Department of Occupational Therapy
1 Washington Square
San Jose, CA 95192-0059
www.sjsu.edu/ot

University of Southern California (M, B/M)
Department of Occupational Science and Occupational Therapy
1540 Alcazar, CHP-133
Los Angeles, CA 90089-9003
www.usc.edu/ot

Colorado

Colorado State University (M)
Department of Occupational Therapy
224 Occupational Therapy Bldg.
Fort Collins, CO 80523-1573
www.cahs.colostate.edu/ot

Connecticut

Quinnipiac University (B/M)
Department of Occupational Therapy
School of Health Sciences
275 Mount Carmel Ave.
Hamden, CT 06518-0569
www.quinnipiac.edu

Sacred Heart University (M)
Program in Occupational Therapy
5151 Park Ave.
Fairfield, CT 06432-1000
www.sacredheart.edu

District of Columbia

Howard University (M)
Department of Occupational Therapy
Division of Allied Health Sciences
6th and Bryant Sts. NW
Washington, DC 20059-0001
www.howard.edu

Florida

Barry University (M)
Occupational Therapy Program
11300 NE 2nd Ave.
Miami Shores, FL 33161-6695
www.barry.edu/snhs/msprograms/occupationaltherapy

Florida Agricultural and Mechanical University (M)
Division of Occupational Therapy
Ware-Rhaney Bldg. East, Rm. 318
Tallahassee, FL 32307-3500
www.famu.edu

Florida Gulf Coast University (M)
Department of Occupational Therapy and Community Health
10501 FGCU Blvd. South
Fort Myers, FL 33965-6565
www.fgcu.edu/chp/ot

Florida International University (M, B/M)
Department of Occupational Therapy
University Park Campus, HLS 237
Miami, FL 33199
www.ot.fiu.edu

Nova Southeastern University (M, P)
Occupational Therapy Department
Health Professions Division, College of Allied Health and Nursing
3200 S. University Dr.
Ft. Lauderdale, FL 33328-2018
www.nova.edu/ot

University of Florida (M)
Department of Occupational Therapy
P.O. Box 100164, HSC
Gainesville, FL 32610-0164
www.phhp.ufl.edu/ot

University of St. Augustine for Health Sciences (M, P)
Institute of Occupational Therapy
1 University Blvd.
St. Augustine, FL 32086-5783
www.usa.edu

Georgia

Brenau University (M, B/M)
Occupational Therapy Department
500 Washington St. SE
Gainesville, GA 30501
www.brenau.edu

Medical College of Georgia (M)
School of Allied Health Sciences
Department of Occupational Therapy
1120 15th St.
Augusta, GA 30912-0700
www.mcg.edu/sah/ot/index.html

Medical College of Georgia at Columbus State University (M)
Occupational Therapy Program
Illges Hall, Rm. 107
4225 University Ave.
Columbus, GA 31907-5645
www.mcg.edu/sah/ot/index.html

Idaho

Idaho State University (M, B/M)
Occupational Therapy Program
Campus Box 8045
Pocatello, ID 83209-8045
www.isu.edu/departments/dpot

Illinois

Chicago State University (M, B/M)
Occupational Therapy Program
College of Health Sciences
9501 S. King Dr.
Chicago, IL 60628-1598
www.csu.edu

Governors State University (M)
Occupational Therapy Program
College of Health Professions
University Park, IL 60466-0975
www.govst.edu

Midwestern University (M)
Occupational Therapy Program
College of Health Sciences
555 31st St.
Downers Grove, IL 60515-1235
www.midwestern.edu

Rush University (M)
Department of Occupational Therapy
Rush University Medical Center
600 S. Paulina, Ste. 1011
Chicago, IL 60612-3833
www.rushu.rush.edu/occuth

University of Illinois at Chicago (M)
Department of Occupational Therapy
College of Applied Health Sciences
1919 W. Taylor St., M/C 811
Chicago, IL 60612-7250
www.ahs.uic.edu/ahs/php/index.php?sitename=ot

Indiana

Indiana University (M)
Department of Occupational Therapy
School of Health & Rehabilitation Sciences
Coleman Hall 311
1140 W. Michigan St.
Indianapolis, IN 46202-5119
www.iupui.edu/it/iusahs

University of Indianapolis (M)
School of Occupational Therapy
1400 E. Hanna Ave.
Indianapolis, IN 46227-3697
http://ot.uindy.edu

University of Southern Indiana (B/M)
Occupational Therapy Program
8600 University Blvd.
Evansville, IN 47712-3534
http://health.usi.edu/acadprog/ot/index.htm

Iowa

St. Ambrose University (M)
Occupational Therapy Program
518 W. Locust
Davenport, IA 52803-2898
www.sau.edu/ot

Kansas

University of Kansas Medical Center (B/M)
Department of Occupational Therapy
3901 Rainbow Blvd.
Kansas City, KS 66160-7602
www.kumc.edu

Kentucky

Eastern Kentucky University (M, B/M)
Department of Occupational Therapy
Dizney Bldg.
Richmond, KY 40475-3135
www.ot.eku.edu

Spalding University (M, B/M)
Auerbach School of Occupational Therapy
851 S. 4th St.
Louisville, KY 40203-2188
www.spalding.edu/occupationaltherapy

Louisiana

Louisiana State University Health Sciences Center (M)
Department of Occupational Therapy
School of Allied Health Professions
1900 Gravier St.
New Orleans, LA 70112-2223
http://alliedhealth.lsuhsc.edu/occupationaltherapy

Louisiana State University Health Sciences Center (M)
Program in Occupational Therapy
Department of Rehabilitation Sciences
1501 Kings Hwy.
Shreveport, LA 71130-3932
www.sh.lsuhsc.edu/ah

University of Louisiana (M)
Department of Occupational Therapy
College of Health Sciences
700 University Ave.
Monroe, LA 71209-0430
www.ulm.edu

Maine

Husson College (M)
Occupational Therapy Program
1 College Circle
Bangor, ME 04401-2999
http://depts.husson.edu/ot

Lewiston-Auburn College (M)
University of Southern Maine
Occupational Therapy Program
51 Westminster St.
Lewiston, ME 04240-3534
www.usm.maine.edu/lac/ot

University of New England (B/M)
Occupational Therapy Department
11 Hills Beach Rd.
Biddeford, ME 04005-9599
www.une.edu/chp/ot

Maryland

Towson University (M, B/M)
Department of Occupational Therapy and Occupational Science
8000 York Rd.
Towson, MD 21252-0001
www.towson.edu/ot

Massachusetts

American International College (M, B/M)
Division of Occupational Therapy
1000 State St.
Springfield, MA 01109-3189
www.aic.edu

Bay Path College (M, B/M)
Occupational Therapy Program
588 Longmeadow St.
Longmeadow, MA 01106-2212
www.baypath.edu

Boston University (M, B/M)
Sargent College of Health and Rehabilitation Sciences
Programs in Occupational Therapy
Department of Rehabilitation Sciences
635 Commonwealth Ave.
Boston, MA 02215-1605
www.bu.edu/sargent

Salem State College (B/M)
Occupational Therapy Program
352 Lafayette St.
Salem, MA 01970-5353
www.salemstate.edu

Springfield College (M, B/M)
Occupational Therapy Department
263 Alden St.
Springfield, MA 01109-3797
www.springfieldcollege.edu/ot

Tufts University (M)
Boston School of Occupational Therapy
Department of Occupational Therapy
26 Winthrop St.
Medford, MA 02155-7084
www.tufts.edu

Worcester State College (M, B/M)
Occupational Therapy Department
486 Chandler St.
Worcester, MA 01602-259
www.worcester.edu

Michigan

Baker College of Flint (B/M)
Occupational Therapy Program
G-1050 W. Bristol Rd.
Flint, MI 48507-5508
www.baker.edu

Eastern Michigan University (M, B/M)
Occupational Therapy Program
School of Health Sciences
362 Marshall
Ypsilanti, MI 48197-2239
www.emich.edu

Grand Valley State University (M)
Occupational Therapy Program
School of Health Professions
301 Michigan St. NE, Ste. 200
Grand Rapids, MI 49503-3314
www.gvsu.edu/ot

Saginaw Valley State University (M)
Occupational Therapy Program
Ryder Center West, Rm. 106
7400 Bay Rd.
University Center, MI 48710-0001
www.svsu.edu

Wayne State University (M)
Occupational Therapy Program
Eugene Applebaum College of Pharmacy and Health Sciences
Detroit, MI 48202-3489
www.cphs.wayne.edu/ot

Western Michigan University (M, B/M)
Department of Occupational Therapy
EWB Bldg.
1903 W. Michigan Ave.
Kalamazoo, MI 49008-5051
www.wmich.edu

Minnesota

College of St. Catherine (M, B/M)
Department of Occupational Science and Occupational Therapy
2004 Randolph Ave. (Mail #4092)
St. Paul, MN 55105-1794
www.stkate.edu/ot

College of St. Scholastica (M, B/M)
Occupational Therapy Department
1200 Kenwood Ave.
Duluth, MN 55811-4199
www.css.edu

University of Minnesota (M)
Program in Occupational Therapy
MMC 388
420 Delaware St. SE
Minneapolis, MN 55455-0392
www.ot.umn.edu

Mississippi

University of Mississippi Medical Center (B/M)
Department of Occupational Therapy
School of Health Related Professions
2500 N. State St.
Jackson, MS 39216-4505
http://shrp.umc.edu

Missouri

Maryville University (M)
Occupational Therapy Program
13550 Conway Rd.
St. Louis, MO 63141
www.maryville.edu

Rockhurst University (M)
Occupational Therapy Program
College of Graduate and Professional Studies
1100 Rockhurst Rd.
Kansas City, MO 64110-2561
www.rockhurst.edu/ot

St. Louis University (M, B/M)
Department of Occupational Science and Occupational Therapy
Edward & Margaret Doisy School of Allied Health Professions
3437 Caroline St.
St. Louis, MO 63104-111
www.slu.edu/doisycollege/osot

University of Missouri (M)
Department of Occupational Therapy
School of Health Professions
407 Lewis Hall
Columbia, MO 65211-4240
www.umshp.org/ot

Washington University (M, P)
Program in Occupational Therapy
School of Medicine
4444 Forest Park Ave., Campus Box 8505
St. Louis, MO 63108
www.ot.wustl.edu

Nebraska

College of St. Mary (B/M)
Occupational Therapy Program
Division of Health Care Professions
7000 Mercy Rd.
Omaha, NE 68106-2377
www.csm.edu

Creighton University (P)
Department of Occupational Therapy
School of Pharmacy and Health Professions
2500 California Plaza
Omaha, NE 68178-0259
http://ot.creighton.edu

New Hampshire

University of New Hampshire (M, B/M)
Occupational Therapy Department
School of Health and Human Services
Hewitt Hall, 4 Library Way
Durham, NH 03824-3563
www.shhs.unh.edu/ot

New Jersey

Kean University (M, B/M)
Occupational Therapy Department
College of Natural, Applied, and Health Sciences
1000 Morris Ave., T-209
Union, NJ 07083-9982
www.kean.edu/~ot

Richard Stockton College of New Jersey (M)
Occupational Therapy Program, Professional Studies Division
P.O. Box 195
Pomona, NJ 08240-0195
www.stockton.edu

Seton Hall University (M, B/M)
Occupational Therapy Program
McQuaid Hall
400 South Orange Ave.
South Orange, NJ 07079-2689
http://gradmeded.shu.edu/prog_master_occupational_therapy.htm

New Mexico

University of New Mexico (M)
Health Sciences Center
Occupational Therapy Graduate Program
MSC09 5240
1 University of New Mexico
Albuquerque, NM 87131-0001
http://hsc.unm.edu//som/ot

New York

Columbia University (M)
Programs in Occupational Therapy
Neurological Institute, 8th Fl.
710 W. 168th St.
New York, NY 10032-2603
http://columbiaot.org

Dominican College (M, B/M)
Occupational Therapy Program
470 Western Hwy.
Orangeburg, NY 10962-1299
www.dc.edu

D'Youville College (M, B/M)
Occupational Therapy Department
1 D'Youville Square
320 Porter Ave.
Buffalo, NY 14201-1084
www.dyc.edu

Ithaca College (B/M)
Department of Occupational Therapy
206 Smiddy Hall
Ithaca, NY 14850-7079
www.ithaca.edu/hshp/ot

Keuka College (B/M)
Division of Occupational Therapy
Keuka Park, NY 14478-0098
www.keuka.edu

Long Island University (B/M)
Division of Occupational Therapy
1 University Plaza, HS Rm. 512
Brooklyn, NY 11201-5372
www.liu.edu

Mercy College (M, B/M)
Occupational Therapy Program
555 Broadway
Dobbs Ferry, NY 10522-1134
http://grad.mercy.edu/occupationaltherapy

New York Institute of Technology (M, B/M)
Department of Occupational Therapy
Northern Blvd.
Riland Bldg., Rm. 351
Old Westbury, NY 11568-8000
www.nyit.edu

New York University (M)
Department of Occupational Therapy
35 W. 4th St., 11th Fl.
New York, NY 10012-1172
www.education.nyu.edu/ot

Sage Colleges (M, B/M)
Occupational Therapy Program
45 Ferry St.
Troy, NY 12180-4115
www.sage.edu

State University of New York
Downstate Medical Center (M)
Occupational Therapy Program
450 Clarkson Ave., Box 81
Brooklyn, NY 11203-2098
www.downstate.edu/chrp/ot

Stony Brook University (B/M)
Occupational Therapy Program
School of Health Technology and Management, L2-HSC
Division of Rehabilitation Sciences
Stony Brook, NY 11794-8201
www.sunysb.edu

Touro College (B/M)
Occupational Therapy Program
1700 Union Blvd.
Bay Shore, NY 11706-7928
www.touro.edu/shs

Touro College–Manhattan (B/M)
Occupational Therapy Program
27–33 W. 23rd St.
New York, NY 10010-4202
www.touro.edu/shs

University at Buffalo, State University of New York (B/M)
Program in Occupational Therapy
Department of Rehabilitation Science
515 Stockton Kimball Tower, 3435 Main St.
Buffalo, NY 14214-3079
http://phhp.buffalo.edu/rs/ot

Utica College (M)
Occupational Therapy Program
Division of Health and Human Studies
1600 Burrstone Rd.
Utica, NY 13502-4892
www.utica.edu

York College, City University of New York (B/M)
Occupational Therapy Program
94-20 Guy R. Brewer Blvd.
Jamaica, NY 11451-9902
www.york.cuny.edu

North Carolina

East Carolina University (M)
Occupational Therapy Department
School of Allied Health Sciences
Greenville, NC 27858-4353
www.ecu.edu/ot

Lenoir-Rhyne College (M, B/M)
Occupational Therapy Program
Box 7547
Hickory, NC 28603-7547
www.lrc.edu/ot

University of North Carolina (M)
Division of Occupational Science
Medical School, Wing E, CB #7120
Chapel Hill, NC 27599-7120
www.alliedhealth.unc.edu/ocsci

Winston-Salem State University (M)
Occupational Therapy Program
601 Martin Luther King Jr. Dr.
Winston-Salem, NC 27110-0003
www.wssu.edu

North Dakota

University of Mary (M)
Occupational Therapy Program
7500 University Dr.
Bismarck, ND 58504-9652
www.umary.edu

University of North Dakota (M)
Department of Occupational Therapy
Box 7126
Grand Forks, ND 58202-7126
www.med.und.nodak.edu/depts/ot

Ohio

Cleveland State University (M)
Occupational Therapy Program
Health Sciences (HS) 103
2121 Euclid Ave.
Cleveland, OH 44115-2440
www.csuohio.edu/healthsci/hs.htm

Medical University of Ohio (P)
Department of Occupational Therapy
School of Allied Health
3015 Arlington Ave.
Toledo, OH 43614-5803
www.meduohio.edu

Ohio State University (M)
Occupational Therapy Division
School of Allied Medical Professions
406 Atwell Hall
453 W. 10th Ave.
Columbus, OH 43210-1234
www.osu.edu

Shawnee State University (M)
Occupational Therapy Program
940 Second St.
Portsmouth, OH 45662-4303
www.shawnee.edu

University of Findlay (B/M)
Occupational Therapy Program
1000 N. Main St.
Findlay, OH 45840-3695
www.findlay.edu

Xavier University (M, B/M)
Department of Occupational Therapy
3800 Victory Pkwy.
Cincinnati, OH 45207-7341
www.xavier.edu/ot_grad

Oklahoma

University of Oklahoma Health Sciences Center (M)
Department of Occupational Therapy
College of Allied Health
801 NE 13th St.
Oklahoma City, OK 73104-5072
www.ah.ouhsc.edu/main/programs/progbrief.asp?prog_id=7

University of Oklahoma at Schusterman Health
    Sciences Center (M)
Department of Occupational Therapy
4502 E. 41st St.
Tulsa, OK 74135-2512
www.ah.ouhsc.edu/main/programs/progbrief.asp?prog_id=7

Oregon

Pacific University (M)
School of Occupational Therapy
2043 College Way
Forest Grove, OR 97116-1797
www.ot.pacificu.edu

Pennsylvania

Alvernia College (M, B/M)
Occupational Therapy Program
400 Saint Bernardine St.
Reading, PA 19607-1799
www.alvernia.edu

Chatham College (M, B/M)
Occupational Therapy Program
Woodland Rd.
Pittsburgh, PA 15232-2826
www.chatham.edu/ot

College Misericordia (M, B/M)
Occupational Therapy Program
Division of Health Sciences
301 Lake St.
Dallas, PA 18612-1098
www.misericordia.edu

Duquesne University (M, B/M)
Department of Occupational Therapy
John G. Rangos Sr. School of Health Sciences, Rm. 234
Pittsburgh, PA 15282-0020
www.healthsciences.duq.edu/ot/othome.html

Elizabethtown College (B/M)
Department of Occupational Therapy
1 Alpha Dr.
Elizabethtown, PA 17022-2298
www.etown.edu

Gannon University (M, B/M)
Occupational Therapy Program
109 University Square
Erie, PA 16541-0001
www.gannon.edu

Philadelphia University (M)
Occupational Therapy Program
School House La. & Henry Ave.
Philadelphia, PA 19144-5497
www.philau.edu/ot

St. Francis University (M, B/M)
Occupational Therapy Program
P.O. Box 600
Loretto, PA 15940-0600
www.saintfrancisuniversity.edu

Temple University (M)
Department of Occupational Therapy
College of Health Professions
3307 N. Broad St.
Philadelphia, PA 19140-5101
www.temple.edu/ot

Thomas Jefferson University (M, B/M)
Department of Occupational Therapy
Jefferson College of Health Professions
Edison Bldg., Rm. 810
130 S. 9th St.
Philadelphia, PA 19107-5233
www.jefferson.edu/jchp/ot/index.cfm

University of Pittsburgh (M)
Department of Occupational Therapy
School of Health and Rehabilitation Sciences
5012 Forbes Tower
Pittsburgh, PA 15260
www.shrs.pitt.edu/ot/index.html

University of the Sciences in Philadelphia (M, B/M)
Department of Occupational Therapy
600 S. 43rd St., Box 24
Philadelphia, PA 19104-4495
www.usip.edu

University of Scranton (B/M)
Occupational Therapy Department
800 Linden St., Leahy Hall
Scranton, PA 18510-4586
www.scranton.edu

Puerto Rico

University of Puerto Rico (M)
Occupational Therapy Program
Medical Sciences Campus-CHRP
P.O. Box 365067
San Juan, PR 00936-5067
www.upr.clu.edu

South Carolina

Medical College of South Carolina (M)
Occupational Therapy Educational Program
College of Health Professions
151 Rutledge Ave., Bldg. B
P.O. Box 250965
Charleston, SC 29425-0965
www.musc.edu/chp/ot

South Dakota

University of South Dakota (M)
Department of Occupational Therapy
414 E. Clark St.
Vermillion, SD 57069-2390
www.usd.edu/usdot

Tennessee

Belmont University (M, P)
School of Occupational Therapy
1900 Belmont Blvd.
Nashville, TN 37212-3757
www.belmont.edu/ot

Milligan College (M)
Occupational Therapy Program
P.O. Box 130
Milligan College, TN 37682
www.milligan.edu

Tennessee State University (M)
Occupational Therapy Department
School of Allied Health Professions
3500 John Merritt Blvd.
Nashville, TN 37209-1561
www.tnstate.edu/ot

University of Tennessee Health Science Center (M)
Department of Occupational Therapy
College of Allied Health Sciences
930 Madison, Ste. 663
Memphis, TN 38163-0002
www.utmem.edu/occ_therapy/home.htmo

Texas

Texas Tech University Health Sciences Center (M)
Occupational Therapy Program
3601 4th St., STOP 6220
Lubbock, TX 79430-6220
www.ttuhsc.edu

Texas Woman's University (M)
School of Occupational Therapy
8194 Walnut Hill La.
Dallas, TX 75231-4365
www.twu.edu/ot

Texas Woman's University (M, B/M)
School of Occupational Therapy
Box 425648, TWU Station
Denton, TX 76204-5648
www.twu.edu/ot

Texas Woman's University (M)
School of Occupational Therapy
1130 John Freeman Blvd.
Houston, TX 77030
www.twu.edu.ot

University of Texas (M)
Occupational Therapy Program
College of Health Sciences
1101 N. Campbell St.
El Paso, TX 79902-4299
www.utep.edu

University of Texas Health Science Center (B/M)
Department of Occupational Therapy
7703 Floyd Curl Dr., Mail Code 6245
San Antonio, TX 78229-3900
www.uthscsa.edu

University of Texas Medical Branch (M)
Department of Occupational Therapy
School of Allied Health Sciences
301 University Blvd.
Galveston, TX 77555-1142
www.sahs.utmb.edu/programs/ot

University of Texas Pan-American (M)
Occupational Therapy Program
1201 W. University Dr.
Edinburg, TX 78539-2999
www.panam.edu

Utah

University of Utah (M)
Division of Occupational Therapy
520 Wakara Way
Salt Lake City, UT 84108-1290
www.health.utah.edu/octh

Virginia

James Madison University (M, B/M)
Occupational Therapy Program
Department of Health Sciences
College of Integrated Science and Technology, MSC 4301
701 Carrier Dr.
Harrisonburg, VA 22807-0001
www.healthsci.jmu.edu/occupationaltherapy

Jefferson College of Health Sciences (M)
Occupational Therapy Program
920 S. Jefferson St.
Roanoke, VA 24016
www.jchs.edu

Shenandoah University (M, B/M)
Occupational Therapy Program
333 W. Cork St., Ste. 510
Winchester, VA 22601-5195
www.su.edu/ot

Virginia Commonwealth University (M)
Department of Occupational Therapy
1000 E. Marshall St.
P.O. Box 980008
Richmond, VA 23298-0008
www.sahp.vcu.edu/occu

Washington

Eastern Washington University (M)
Department of Occupational Therapy
Health Sciences Bldg., Rm. 225C, Box R
310 N. Riverpoint Blvd.
Spokane, WA 99004-1675
www.ewu.edu/x3369.xml

University of Puget Sound (M)
Occupational Therapy Program
School of Occupational Therapy
1500 N. Warner
Tacoma, WA 98416-1070
www.ups.edu/ot

University of Washington (M)
Division of Occupational Therapy
Department of Rehabilitation Medicine
Box 356490
Seattle, WA 98195-6490
http://depts.washington.edu/rehab/ot

West Virginia

West Virginia University (M)
Division of Occupational Therapy
P.O. Box 9139
Morgantown, WV 26506-9139
www.hsc.wvu.edu/som/ot

Wisconsin

Concordia University Wisconsin (M, B/M)
Occupational Therapy Program
12800 N. Lake Shore Dr.
Mequon, WI 53092-2402
www2.cuw.edu

Mount Mary College (M, B/M)
Occupational Therapy Department
2900 N. Menomonee River Pkwy.
Milwaukee, WI 53222-4597
www.mtmary.edu

University of Wisconsin–La Crosse (M)
Occupational Therapy Program
4049 Health Science Center
1725 State St.
La Crosse, WI 54601-9959
www.uwlax.com

University of Wisconsin–Madison (M)
Occupational Therapy Program
1300 University Ave. (2110/MSC)
Madison, WI 53706-1532
www.education.wisc.edu/kinesiology/ot

University of Wisconsin–Milwaukee (B,M)
Occupational Therapy Program
College of Health Sciences
P.O. Box 413
Milwaukee, WI 53201-0413
www.uwm.edu/chs

Wyoming

University of North Dakota at Casper College (M)
125 College Dr.
Casper, WY 82601-9958
www.med.und.nodak.edu/depts/ot

Occupational Therapy Assistant Programs

All of the programs listed below offer associate degrees in occupational therapy, unless otherwise noted.

Alabama

Wallace State Community College
Occupational Therapy Assistant Program
P.O. Box 2000
Hanceville, AL 35077-2000
www.wallacestate.edu/ota

Arkansas

South Arkansas Community College
Occupational Therapy Assistant Program
P.O. Box 7010
300 South West Ave.
El Dorado, AR 71731-7010
www.southark.edu

California

Grossmont College
Occupational Therapy Assistant Program
8800 Grossmont College Dr.
El Cajon, CA 92020-1799
www.grossmont.net/healthprofessions

Loma Linda University
Occupational Therapy Assistant Program
Nichol Hall, Rm. A912
Loma Linda, CA 92350-0001
www.llu.edu/llu/sahp

Sacramento City College
Occupational Therapy Assistant Program
Science and Allied Health Division
3835 Freeport Blvd.
Sacramento, CA 95822-1386
www.scc.losrios.edu

Santa Ana College
Occupational Therapy Assistant Program
1530 W. 17th St.
Santa Ana, CA 92706-3398
www.sac.edu

Colorado

Pueblo Community College
Occupational Therapy Assistant Program
900 W. Orman Ave.
Pueblo, CO 81004-1499
www.pueblocc.edu

Connecticut

Briarwood College
Occupational Therapy Assistant Program
2279 Mount Vernon Rd.
Southington, CT 06489
www.briarwoodcollege.com

Housatonic Community-Technical College
Occupational Therapy Assistant Program
900 Lafayette Blvd.
Bridgeport, CT 06604-4704
www.hctc.commnet.edu

Manchester Community College
Occupational Therapy Assistant Program
Great Path, M.S. #17
P.O. Box 1046
Manchester, CT 06045-1046
www.mcc.commnet.edu

Delaware

Delaware Technical and Community College–Owens Campus
Occupational Therapy Assistant Program
P.O. Box 610
Georgetown, DE 19947-0610
www.dtcc.edu

Delaware Technical and Community College–Wilmington Campus
Occupational Therapy Assistant Program
333 Shipley St.
Wilmington, DE 19801-2499
www.dtcc.edu/wilmington/ah

Florida

Daytona Beach Community College
Occupational Therapy Assistant Program
1200 International Speedway Blvd.
Daytona Beach, FL 32120-2811
www.dbcc.edu

Florida Hospital College of Health Sciences
Occupational Therapy Assistant Program
711 Lake Estelle Dr.
Orlando, FL 32803-1235
www.fhchs.edu

Keiser College
Occupational Therapy Assistant Program
1500 NW 49th St.
Ft. Lauderdale, FL 33309
www.keisercollege.edu

Keiser College–Melbourne Campus
Occupational Therapy Assistant Program
900 S. Babcock St.
Melbourne, FL 32901
www.keisercollege.edu

Manatee Community College
Occupational Therapy Assistant Program
5840 26th St. West, Bldg. 28
Bradenton, FL 34207-7046
www.mccfl.edu

Polk Community College
Occupational Therapy Assistant Program
Math, Science, and Health Division
999 Ave. H NE
Winter Haven, FL 33881-4299
www.polk.edu

Georgia

Augusta Technical College
Occupational Therapy Assistant Program
3200 Augusta Tech Dr.
Augusta, GA 30906-3399
www.augusta.tec.ga.us

Darton College
Occupational Therapy Assistant Program
2400 Gillionville Rd.
Albany, GA 31707-3098
www.darton.edu/programs

Middle College Georgia
Occupational Therapy Assistant Program
1100 2nd St. SE
Cochran, GA 31014-1599
www.mgc.edu

Northwestern Technical College
Occupational Therapy Assistant Program
265 Bicentennial Trail
P.O. Box 569
Rock Spring, GA 30739
www.northwesterntech.edu

Hawaii

University of Hawaii
Kapiolani Community College
Occupational Therapy Assistant Program
Health Sciences Department
4303 Diamond Head Rd., Kauila 210 C
Honolulu, HI 96816-4421
www.kcc.hawaii.edu

Idaho

Kirkwood Community College
Occupational Therapy Assistant Program
6301 Kirkwood Blvd. SW
Cedar Rapids, IA 52406-9973
www.kirkwood.edu

Illinois

Illinois Central College
Occupational Therapy Assistant Program
201 SW Adams
Peoria, IL 61635-0001
www.icc.edu

Lewis and Clark Community College
Occupational Therapy Assistant Program
5800 Godfrey Rd.
Godfrey, IL 62035-2466
www.lc.edu

Lincoln Land Community College
Occupational Therapy Assistant Program
5250 Shepherd Rd.
Box 19256
Springfield, IL 62794-9256
www.llcc.edu

Parkland College
Occupational Therapy Assistant Program
2400 W. Bradley Ave.
Champaign, IL 61821-1899
www.parkland.edu

South Suburban College of Cook County
Occupational Therapy Assistant Program
15800 S. State St.
South Holland, IL 60473-1262
www.southsuburbancollege.edu

Southern Illinois Collegiate Common Market
Occupational Therapy Assistant Program
3213 S. Park Ave.
Herrin, IL 62948-3711
www.siccm.com

Wright College
Occupational Therapy Assistant Program
4300 N. Narragansett Ave.
Chicago, IL 60634-1591
http://wright.ccc.edu/department/ota/index.asp

Indiana

University of Southern Indiana
Occupational Therapy Assistant Department
School of Nursing and Health Professions
8600 University Blvd.
Evansville, IN 47712-3534
http://health.usi.edu/acadprog/ota/index.htm

Kentucky

Jefferson Community and Technical College
Occupational Therapy Assistant Program
Downtown Campus
109 E. Broadway
Louisville, KY 40202-2005
www.jefferson.kctcs.edu

Madisonville Community College
Occupational Therapy Assistant Program
750 N. Laffoon St.
Madisonville, KY 42431-1636
www.madcc.kctcs.edu

Louisiana

Delgado Community College
Occupational Therapy Assistant Program
City Park Campus
615 City Park Ave.
New Orleans, LA 70119-4399
www.dcc.edu

University of Louisiana at Monroe
Occupational Therapy Assistant Program
College of Health Sciences
Monroe, LA 71209-0430
www.ulm.edu

Maine

Kennebec Valley Community College
Occupational Therapy Assistant Program
92 Western Ave.
Fairfield, ME 04937-1367
www.kvcc.me.edu

Maryland

Allegany College of Maryland
Occupational Therapy Assistant Program
12401 Willowbrook Rd. SE
Cumberland, MD 21502-2596
www.allegany.edu

Community College of Baltimore County at Catonsville
Occupational Therapy Assistant Program
800 S. Rolling Rd.
Catonsville, MD 21228-9987
www.ccbcmd.edu

Massachusetts

Bristol Community College
Occupational Therapy Assistant Program
777 Elsbree St.
Fall River, MA 02720-9960
www.bristol.mass.edu

North Shore Community College
Occupational Therapy Assistant Program
1 Ferncroft Rd.
Danvers, MA 01923-0840
www.northshore.edu

Quinsigamond Community College
Occupational Therapy Assistant Program
670 W. Boylston St.
Worcester, MA 01606-2092
www.qcc.mass.edu

Springfield Technical Community College
Occupational Therapy Assistant Program
1 Armory Sq., Ste. 1
P.O. Box 9000
Springfield, MA 01102-9000
www.stcc.edu

Michigan

Baker College of Muskegon
Occupational Therapy Assistant Program
1903 Marquette Ave.
Muskegon, MI 49442-1490
www.baker.edu

Charles Stewart Mott Community College
Occupational Therapy Assistant Program
Southern Lakes Branch Campus
2100 W. Thompson Rd.
Fenton, MI 48430-9798
www.mcc.edu

Grand Rapids Community College
Occupational Therapy Assistant Program
143 Bostwick NE
Grand Rapids, MI 49503-3295
www.grcc.cc.mi.us

Macomb Community College
Occupational Therapy Assistant Program
Bldg. E-220-8
44575 Garfield Rd.
Clinton Township, MI 48038-1139
www.macomb.edu

Wayne County Community College District
Occupational Therapy Assistant Program
1001 W. Fort St.
Detroit, MI 48226-9975
www.wcccd.edu

Minnesota

Annoka Technical College
Occupational Therapy Assistant Program
1355 W. Highway 10
Anoka, MN 55303-1590
www.ank.tec.mn.us

College of St. Catherine–Minneapolis
Occupational Therapy Assistant Program
601 25th Ave. South
Minneapolis, MN 55454-1494
http://minerva.stkate.edu/offices/academic/ota.nsf

Northland Community and Technical College
Occupational Therapy Assistant Program
2022 Central Ave. NE
East Grand Forks, MN 56721-2702
www.northlandcollege.edu

Mississippi

Holmes Community College
Occupational Therapy Assistant Program
412 W. Ridgeland Ave.
Ridgeland, MS 39157
www.holmescc.edu

Pearl River Community College
Occupational Therapy Assistant Program
5448 U.S. Hwy. 49 South
Hattiesburg, MS 39401-7806
www.prcc.edu

Missouri

Metropolitan Community College
Occupational Therapy Assistant Program
3201 Southwest Trafficway
Kansas City, MO 64111-2764
www.kcmetro.edu

Ozarks Technical Community College
Occupational Therapy Assistant Program
1001 E. Chestnut Expy.
Springfield, MO 65802
www.otc.edu

Sanford-Brown College
Occupational Therapy Assistant Program
Hazelwood Campus
75 Village Square
Hazelwood, MO 63042
www.sanford-brown.edu

St. Charles County Community College
Occupational Therapy Assistant Program
4601 Mid Rivers Mall Dr.
Cottleville, MO 63376-2865
www.stchas.edu

St. Louis Community College–Meramec
Occupational Therapy Assistant Program
11333 Big Bend Blvd.
St. Louis, MO 63122-5799
www.stlcc.edu

Nevada

Community College of Southern Nevada–West Charleston Campus
Occupational Therapy Assistant Program
6375 W. Charleston Blvd., W1A
Las Vegas, NV 89146-1139
www.ccsn.nevada.edu/health/ota.htm

New Hampshire

New Hampshire Community Technical College
Occupational Therapy Assistant Program
1 College Dr.
Claremont, NH 03743-9707
www.claremont.nhctc.edu

New Mexico

Eastern New Mexico University
Occupational Therapy Assistant Program
P.O. Box 6000
Roswell, NM 88202-6000
www.roswell.enmu.edu

Western New Mexico University
Occupational Therapy Assistant Program
P.O. Box 680
Silver City, NM 88062-0680
www.wnmu.edu

New York

Erie Community College
Occupational Therapy Assistant Program
North Campus
6205 Main St.
Williamsville, NY 14221-7095
www.ecc.edu

Genesee Community College
Occupational Therapy Assistant Program
1 College Rd.
Batavia, NY 14020-9704
www.genesee.edu

Jamestown Community College
Occupational Therapy Assistant Program
525 Falconer St.
Jamestown, NY 14702-0020
www.sunyjcc.edu

LaGuardia Community College
Occupational Therapy Assistant Program
31-10 Thomson Ave.
Long Island City, NY 11101-3083
www.lagcc.cuny.edu

Maria College
Occupational Therapy Assistant Program
700 New Scotland Ave.
Albany, NY 12208-1798
www.mariacollege.edu

Mercy College
Occupational Therapy Assistant Program
555 Broadway
Dobbs Ferry, NY 10522-1134
www.mercy.edu

Orange County Community College
Occupational Therapy Assistant Program
115 South St.
Middletown, NY 10940-6404
www.orange.cc.ny.us/ota

Rockland Community College
Occupational Therapy Assistant Program
145 College Rd.
Suffern, NY 10901-3699
www.sunyrockland.edu

State University of New York at Canton
College of Technology
Occupational Therapy Assistant Program
34 Cornell Dr.
Canton, NY 13617-1096
www.canton.edu

Suffolk County Community College
Michael J. Grant Campus
Occupational Therapy Assistant Program
Crooked Hill Rd., MA 308
Brentwood, NY 11717-1092
www.sunysuffolk.edu

Touro College
Occupational Therapy Assistant Program
27–33 W. 23rd St.
New York, NY 10010-4202
www.touro.edu

North Carolina

Cabarrus College of Health Sciences
Occupational Therapy Assistant Program
401 Medical Park Dr.
Concord, NC 28025-2405
www.cabarruscollege.edu

Cape Fear Community College
Occupational Therapy Assistant Program
411 N. Front St.
Wilmington, NC 28401-3993
http://cfcc.edu/ota

Durham Technical Community College
Occupational Therapy Assistant Program
1637 Lawson St.
Durham, NC 27703-5023
www.durhamtech.edu

Pitt Community College
Occupational Therapy Assistant Program
P.O. Drawer 7007
Greenville, NC 27835-7007
http://styx.pitt.cc.nc.us/division/department/occtherapy/index.html

North Dakota

North Dakota State College of Science
Occupational Therapy Assistant Program
Mayme Green Allied Health Facility
800 6th St. North
Wahpeton, ND 58076-0002
www.ndscs.nodak.edu

Ohio

Cincinnati State Technical and Community College
Occupational Therapy Assistant Program
3520 Central Pkwy.
Cincinnati, OH 45223-2690
www.cincinnatistate.edu

Cuyahoga Community College
Occupational Therapy Assistant Program
2900 Community College Ave.
Cleveland, OH 44115-3196
www.tri-c.edu/otat

James A. Rhodes State College
Occupational Therapy Assistant Program
4240 Campus Dr.
Lima, OH 45804-3597
www.rhodesstate.edu

Owens Community College
Occupational Therapy Assistant Program
P.O. Box 10000
Toledo, OH 43699-1947
www.owens.edu

Shawnee State University
Occupational Therapy Assistant Program
940 Second St.
Portsmouth, OH 45662-4303
www.shawnee.edu

Sinclair Community College
Occupational Therapy Assistant Program
444 W. Third St.
Dayton, OH 45402-146
www.sinclair.edu/academics/alh/departments/ota

Stark State College of Technology
Occupational Therapy Assistant Program
6200 Frank Ave. NW
Canton, OH 44720-7299
www.starkstate.edu

Zane State College
Occupational Therapy Assistant Program
1555 Newark Rd.
Zanesville, OH 43701-2694
www.zanestate.edu

Oklahoma

Caddo-Kiowa Vocational Technical Center
Southwestern Oklahoma State University
Occupational Therapy Assistant Program
P.O. Box 190
Fort Cobb, OK 73038
www.caddokiowa.com/academics/ota.htm

Oklahoma City Community College
Occupational Therapy Assistant Program
Health Professions Division
7777 S. May Ave.
Oklahoma City, OK 73159-4444
www.okccc.edu/health/ota.html

Tulsa Community College–Metro Campus
Occupational Therapy Assistant Program
909 S. Boston Ave.
Tulsa, OK 74119-2095
www.tulsacc.edu

Pennsylvania

Community College of Allegheny County–Boyce Campus
Occupational Therapy Assistant Program
595 Beatty Rd.
Monroeville, PA 15146-1395
www.ccac.edu

ICM School of Business and Medical Careers
Occupational Therapy Assistant Program
10 Wood St.
Pittsburgh, PA 15222-1977
www.icmschool.com

Lehigh Carbon Community College
Occupational Therapy Assistant Program
4525 Education Park Dr.
Schnecksville, PA 18078-2598
www.lccc.edu

Mount Aloysius College
Occupational Therapy Assistant Program
7373 Admiral Peary Hwy.
Cresson, PA 16630-1999
www.mtaloy.edu

Pennsylvania College of Technology
Occupational Therapy Assistant Program
1 College Ave.
Williamsport, PA 17701-5799
www.pct.edu

Pennsylvania State University
Occupational Therapy Assistant Program
College Pl.
DuBois, PA 15801-3199
www.ds.psu.edu/academics

Pennsylvania State University
Occupational Therapy Assistant Program
1 Campus Dr.
Mont Alto, PA 17237-9703
www.ma.psu.edu

Pennsylvania State University
Berks-Lehigh Valley College
Occupational Therapy Assistant Program
P.O. Box 7009
Reading, PA 19610-6009
www.lv.psu.edu

Puerto Rico

University of Puerto Rico at Humacao
Occupational Therapy Assistant Program
CUH Postal Station 100 Carr. 908
Humacao, PR 00791-4300
www.uprh.edu

Rhode Island

Community College of Rhode Island
Occupational Therapy Assistant Program
1 John H. Chaffee Blvd.
Newport, RI 02840
www.ccri.edu

New England Institute of Technology
Occupational Therapy Assistant Program
2500 Post Rd.
Warwick, RI 02886-2266
www.neit.edu

South Carolina

Greenville Technical College–Greer Campus
Occupational Therapy Assistant Program
506 S. Pleasantburg Dr.
Greenville, SC 29606-5616
www.greenvilletech.com

Trident Technical College
Occupational Therapy Assistant Program
P.O. Box 118067
Charleston, SC 29423-8067
www.tridenttech.edu

South Dakota

Lake Area Technical Institute
Occupational Therapy Assistant Program
230 11th St. NE
Watertown, SD 57201-0730
www.lakeareatech.edu

Tennessee

Nashville State Technical Community College
Occupational Therapy Assistant Program
120 White Bridge Rd., Ste. W-60
Nashville, TN 37209-4515
www.nscc.edu/depart/ot/index.html

Roane State Community College
Occupational Therapy Assistant Program
276 Patton La.
Harriman, TN 37748-5011
www.roanestate.edu

Texas

Amarillo College
Occupational Therapy Assistant Program
P.O. Box 447
Amarillo, TX 79178-0001
www.actx.edu

Army Medical Department Center and School (certificate)
Occupational Therapy Assistant Program
Academy of Health Sciences, ATTN: MCCS-HMO CDR Silva
3151 Scott Rd., Ste. 1230
Fort Sam Houston, TX 78234-6138
www.cs.amedd.army.mil
(Limited to enlisted personnel in the army, navy, army reserves, and
   to DoD civilians)

Austin Community College–Eastview Campus
Occupational Therapy Assistant Program
3401 Webberville Rd.
Austin, TX 78702
www.austincc.edu/ota

Del Mar College
Occupational Therapy Assistant Program
Department of Allied Health
101 Baldwin and Ayers
Corpus Christi, TX 78404-3897
www.delmar.edu

Houston Community College
Occupational Therapy Assistant Program
Coleman Health Science Bldg.
1900 Pressler
Houston, TX 77030-3717
http://secollege.hccs.cc.tx.us/secollege.html

Kingwood College
North Harris Montgomery Community College District
Occupational Therapy Assistant Program
20000 Kingwood Dr.
Kingwood, TX 77339-3801
wwwkc.nhmccd.edu

Laredo Community College
Occupational Therapy Assistant Program
West End Washington St.
Laredo, TX 78040-4395
www.laredo.edu

Navarro College
Occupational Therapy Assistant Program
3200 W. 7th Ave.
Corsicana, TX 75110-4818
www.navarrocollege.edu

Panola College
Occupational Therapy Assistant Program
1109 W. Panola
Carthage, TX 75633-2397
www.panola.edu/instprog-ota.htm

South Texas College
Occupational Therapy Assistant Program
Nursing/Allied Health Division
P.O. Box 9701
McAllen, TX 78501-9701
www.southtexascollege.edu/nah

St. Philip's College
Occupational Therapy Assistant Program
1801 Martin Luther King Dr.
San Antonio, TX 78203-2098
www.accd.edu/spc/spcmain/spc.htm

Tomball College
North Harris Montgomery Community College District
Occupational Therapy Assistant Program
30555 Tomball Pkwy.
Tomball, TX 77375-4036
wwwtc.nhmccd.edu

Utah

Salt Lake Community College
Occupational Therapy Assistant Program
4600 S. Redwood Rd.
Salt Lake City, UT 84130-0808
www.slcc.edu

Virginia

Jefferson College of Health Sciences
Occupational Therapy Assistant Program
920 S. Jefferson St.
Roanoke, VA 24016-4443
www.jchs.edu

Southwest Virginia Community College
Occupational Therapy Assistant Program
P.O. Box SVCC
Richlands, VA 24641-1101
www.sw.edu

Tidewater Community College
Virginia Beach Campus (certificate, developing associate degree)
Occupational Therapy Assistant Program
1700 College Crescent
Virginia Beach, VA 23456-1918
www.tcc.edu

Washington

Green River Community College
Occupational Therapy Assistant Program
12401 SE 320th St.
Auburn, WA 98092-3699
www.greenriver.edu

West Virginia

Mountain State University
Occupational Therapy Assistant Program
School of Health Sciences
P.O. Box 9003
Beckley, WV 25802-2830
www.mountainstate.edu

Wisconsin

Fox Valley Technical College
Occupational Therapy Assistant Program
1825 N. Bluemound Dr.
P.O. Box 2277
Appleton, WI 54912-2277
www.fvtc.edu

Madison Area Technical College
Occupational Therapy Assistant Program
211 N. Carroll St.
Madison, WI 53703-2285
www.matcmadison.edu

Milwaukee Area Technical College
Occupational Therapy Assistant Program
700 W. State St.
Milwaukee, WI 53233-1443
www.matc.edu

Western Wisconsin Technical College
Occupational Therapy Assistant Program
304 6th St. North
La Crosse, WI 54602-0908
wwtc.edu

Wisconsin Indianhead Technical College
Occupational Therapy Assistant Program
2100 Beaser Ave.
Ashland, WI 54806-3699
www.witc.edu

Wyoming

Casper College
Occupational Therapy Assistant Program
125 College Dr.
Casper, WY 82601-9958
www.caspercollege.edu

APPENDIX B

Professional Associations

American Association for Respiratory Care
9425 N. MacArthur Blvd., Ste. 100
Irving, TX 75063-4706
www.aarc.org

American Occupational Therapy Association
4720 Montgomery La.
Bethesda, MD 20824-1220
www.aota.org

American Physical Therapy Association
1111 N. Fairfax St.
Alexandria, VA 22314-1488
www.apta.org

American Therapeutic Recreation Association
1414 Prince St., Ste. 204
Alexandria, VA 22314
www.atra-tr.org

Association for Play Therapy
2100 N. Winery Ave., Ste. 102
Fresno, CA 93703
www.a4pt.org

National Association of Activity Professionals
P.O. Box 5530
Seviervielle, TN 37864
www.thenaap.com

National Therapeutic Recreation Society
22377 Belmont Ridge Rd.
Ashburn, VA 20148
www.nrpa.org

Bibliography

The periodicals and books listed here offer a wealth of information to anyone interested in a career in occupational therapy.

Periodicals

AARC Times: The Magazine for the Respiratory Care Professional
American Association for Respiratory Care
9425 N. MacArthur Blvd., Ste. 100
Irving, TX 75063-4706
www.aarc.org

American Journal of Occupational Therapy
OT Practice
Special interest section quarterly newsletters (for 11 specializations)
American Occupational Therapy Association
4720 Montgomery La.
Bethesda, MD 20824-1220
www.aota.org

For Your Health
Physical Therapy
PT—Magazine of Physical Therapy
American Physical Therapy Association
1111 N. Fairfax St.
Alexandria, VA 22314-1488
www.apta.org

Canadian Journal of Occupational Therapy
Occupational Therapy Now
Canadian Association of Occupational Therapists
CTTC Bldg., Ste. 3400
1125 Colonel By Dr.
Ottawa, ON K1S 5R1
www.caot.ca

Occupational Therapy Books

American Occupational Therapy Association. *Occupational Therapy Practice Framework: Domain and Process.* Bethesda, Md.: American Occupational Therapy Association, 2002.
Breines, Estelle B. *Occupational Therapy Activities from Clay to Computers: Theory and Practice*, 2nd ed. Philadelphia: F.A. Davis Co., 2005.
Case-Smith, Jane. *Occupational Therapy for Children*, 5th ed. Columbus, Ohio: C. V. Mosby, 2004.
Crepeau, Elizabeth B., ed. *Willard and Spackman's Occupational Therapy*, 10th ed. Philadelphia: Lippincott Williams and Wilkins, 2003.

Johnson, Caryn R., Arlene Lorch, and Tina DeAngelis. *The Occupational Therapy Examination Review Guide*, 2nd ed. Philadelphia: F. A. Davis Co., 2001.

Kronenberg, Frank, Salvador Algado, and Nick Pollard. *Occupational Therapy Without Borders: Learning from the Spirit of Survivors*. New York: Churchill Livingstone, 2004.

Miller-Kuhaneck, Heather. *Autism: A Comprehensive Occupational Therapy Approach*, 2nd ed. Bethesda, Md.: American Occupational Therapy Association, 2004.

Paul, Stanley, and David P. Orchanian. *Pocketguide to Assessment in Occupational Therapy*. Clifton Park, N.Y.: Thomson Delmar Learning, 2003.

Trombley, Catherine A., and Mary Vining Radomski. *Occupational Therapy for Physical Disfunction*, 5th ed. Philadelphia: Lippincott Williams and Wilkins, 2002.

Ziviani, Jenny, ed. *Occupational Therapy with Children: Understanding Children's Occupations*. Oxford: Blackwell Publishing, 2006.

General Job Search Books

Beatty, Richard H. *The Perfect Cover Letter*, 3rd ed. New York: John Wiley & Sons, 2003.

Bolles, Richard N. *What Color Is Your Parachute? 2005: A Practical Manual for Job-Hunters and Career-Changers*. Berkeley, Calif.: Ten Speed Press, 2004.

Dikel, Margaret Riley, and Frances E. Roehm. *The Guide to Internet Job Searching 2004-2005*. Chicago: McGraw-Hill, 2004.

McGraw-Hill, eds. *Résumés for Health and Medical Careers*, 3rd ed. Chicago: McGraw-Hill, 2003.

Rosenberg, Arthur, and David Hizer. *The Résumé Handbook: How to Write Outstanding Résumés and Cover Letters for Every Situation*, 4th ed. Avon, Mass.: Adams Media Corp., 2003.

Troutman, Kathryn K. *The Federal Résumé Guidebook*, 3rd ed. Indianapolis: JIST Works, 2004.

Whitcomb, Susan Britton, and Pat Kendall. *e-Résumés: Everything You Need to Know About Using Electronic Résumés to Tap into Today's Hot Job Market.* New York: McGraw-Hill, 2001.

About the Author

Zona Weeks received her B.S. degree in occupational therapy from the University of Wisconsin, an M.S. in educational psychology from Butler University (Indiana), and a Ph.D. in educational psychology from Indiana University. Her clinical experience has been in occupational therapy for physical dysfunction, with primary emphasis on sensorimotor integration as a basis for treatment. She is also a licensed school psychologist, which allows her to combine experience with learning disabilities with occupational therapy evaluations to more fully understand difficulties related to learning, social-emotional functioning, and movement disorders.

Weeks served as a faculty member in occupational therapy at the Indiana University School of Medicine before leaving to establish and become the founding director of two occupational therapy master of science degree programs at the University of Indianapolis: a professional entry-level master's degree program and a post-professional master's degree program.

Professionally, Weeks has been active at state and national levels. She has served as president of the Indiana Occupational Therapy Association and president of the Indiana Allied Health Association. Nationally, in addition to serving on several committees, she has been a regional research consultant for the American Occupational Therapy Foundation, on whose executive board she served, and she has held positions on the editorial review boards of the *American Journal of Occupational Therapy* and the *Occupational Therapy Journal of Research*. She is currently on the editorial review board of *Cognitive Rehabilitation*. She has published several book chapters and journal articles. Weeks has been honored by being named a fellow of the American Occupational Therapy Association.

This edition has been thoroughly revised and updated by Josephine Scanlon, a freelance writer and editor specializing in career topics.